ECDL®

European Computer Driving Licence®

Computer Essentials
IT User Fundamentals
BCS ITQ Level 1

Using Microsoft® Windows® 7

Syllabus Version 1.0

Release ECDL284v3

Published by: CiA Training Ltd
Business & Innovation Centre
Sunderland Enterprise Park
Sunderland
SR5 2TA
United Kingdom

Tel: +44 (0) 191 549 5002
Fax: +44 (0) 191 549 9005

E-mail: info@ciatraining.co.uk
Web: www.ciatraining.co.uk

ISBN: 978-0-85741-041-2

First published 2013.

European Computer Driving Licence, ECDL, International Computer Driving Licence, ICDL, and related logos are all registered Trade Marks of The European Computer Driving Licence Foundation Limited ("ECDL Foundation").

CiA Training Ltd is an entity independent of The British Computer Society using the name BCS, The Chartered Institute for IT ("BCS") and is not associated with ECDL Foundation or BCS in any manner.

This courseware may be used to assist learners to prepare for the ECDL Certification Programme as titled on the courseware. Neither BCS nor **CiA Training Ltd** warrants that the use of this courseware publication will ensure passing of the tests for that ECDL Certification Programme.

This courseware publication has been independently reviewed and approved by BCS as covering the learning objectives for the ECDL Certification Programme.

Confirmation of this approval can be obtained by reviewing www.bcs.org/ecdl.

The material contained in this courseware publication has not been reviewed for technical accuracy and does not guarantee that candidates will pass the test for the ECDL Certification Programme.

Any and all assessment items and/or performance-based exercises contained in this courseware relate solely to this publication and do not constitute or imply certification by BCS or ECDL Foundation in respect of the ECDL Certification Programme or any other ECDL test.

Irrespective of how the material contained in this courseware is deployed, for example in a learning management system (LMS) or a customised interface, nothing should suggest to the candidate that this material constitutes certification or can lead to certification through any other process than official ECDL certification testing.

For details on sitting a test for an ECDL certification programme in the UK, please visit the BCS website at www.bcs.org/ecdl.

Learners using this courseware must be registered with BCS before undertaking a test for ECDL. Without a valid registration, the test(s) cannot be undertaken and no certificate, nor any other form of recognition, can be given to a learner. Registration should be undertaken with BCS at an Approved Centre.

Downloading the Data Files

Data files accompanying this guide allow you to learn and practise new skills without the need for lots of data entry. These files must be downloaded from the Internet. Go to **www.ciatraining.co.uk/data** and follow the simple on-screen instructions.

Your *FastCode* for this guide's data is: **ECDL284**

The data files should be installed in the following location on your computer:

Documents \ DATA FILES \ ECDL \ Computer Essentials

Aims

The aim of this guide is to provide you with the practical skills required to use modern ICT devices safely and securely. You will learn how to use *Windows 7* to work effectively and create, store and manage files.

Objectives

After completing this guide you will be able to:

- Understand key ICT concepts

- Use the main features of the *Windows 7* operating system

- Adjust computer settings

- Understand the main concepts of file management and be able to efficiently organise files and folders so that they are easy to identify and find

- Create, edit, store and print a simple text document

- Use utility software to compress and extract large files, and use antivirus software to protect against computer viruses and other malware

- Appreciate the importance of data security and backing up

- Be aware of important environmental, legal, and health and safety issues that apply to ICT users

Assessment of Knowledge

At the end of this guide is a **Record of Achievement Matrix**. Before the guide is started, it is recommended that you complete the matrix to measure your current level of knowledge. After working through a section, return to and update the **Record of Achievement**. Only when you feel you are competent in all areas should you move on to the next section.

Contents

SECTION 1 BASICS OF ICT **8**

   1 - ICT CONCEPTS 9

   2 - USING ICT SAFELY 10

   3 - YOUR WORKSPACE 12

   4 - COMPUTING HARDWARE 14

   5 - INPUT AND OUTPUT DEVICES 16

   6 - CONNECTING PERIPHERALS 17

   7 - DATA STORAGE 19

   8 - COMPUTING SOFTWARE 21

   9 - SOFTWARE LICENCES 23

   10 - DEVICE PERFORMANCE 24

   11 - REVISION 25

SECTION 2 GETTING STARTED **26**

   12 - STARTING A COMPUTER... 27

   13 - LOGGING ON 28

   14 - THE WINDOWS DESKTOP 29

   15 - THE START MENU 31

   16 - WINDOW LAYOUT 33

   17 - WORKING WITH WINDOWS 35

   18 - CLOSING WINDOWS 37

   19 - STARTING PROGRAMS... 38

   20 - UNRESPONSIVE PROGRAMS 39

   21 - FINDING HELP.. 41

   22 - LOGGING OFF 43

   23 - SHUTTING DOWN WINDOWS... 44

   24 - REVISION 45

SECTION 3 FILES AND FOLDERS **46**

   25 - FILE AND FOLDER NAVIGATION... 47

   26 - FOLDER VIEWS 50

   27 - FILE TYPES AND ICONS 51

   28 - SORTING FILES AND FOLDERS 53

   29 - CREATING NEW FOLDERS 55

   30 - SELECTING ITEMS 56

   31 - COPYING FILES 58

32 - Moving Files 60

33 - Organising Folders 62

34 - Renaming Items 64

35 - Deleting Items 66

36 - The Recycle Bin 67

37 - Item Properties 69

38 - Searching 71

39 - Search Filters 73

40 - Revision 75

SECTION 4 WORKING WITH TEXT **77**

41 - WordPad 78

42 - Entering Text 80

43 - Saving Documents 82

44 - Opening Documents 84

45 - Cut, Copy and Paste 85

46 - Printing Documents 88

47 - Taking Screenshots 90

48 - Recently Used Files 91

49 - Revision 92

SECTION 5 ICONS AND SHORTCUTS **93**

50 - Default Programs 94

51 - Shortcuts 95

52 - Arranging Icons 97

53 - Revision 98

SECTION 6 STORAGE SPACE **99**

54 - Storage Space 100

55 - Accessing Storage Devices 102

56 - Adding Storage Devices 103

57 - Compressing Files 105

58 - Extracting Files 107

59 - Revision 108

SECTION 7 CONTROL PANEL **109**

60 - Control Panel 110

61 - System Information 112

62 - Display Settings 114

63 - Sound Settings 117

64 - DATE AND TIME SETTINGS 119

65 - LANGUAGE SETTINGS 121

66 - WINDOWS FIREWALL 124

67 - WINDOWS UPDATE 126

68 - BACKING UP 128

69 - INSTALLING PROGRAMS 130

70 - UNINSTALLING PROGRAMS 131

71 - REVISION 132

SECTION 8 PRINTERS **133**

72 - PRINTING 134

73 - PRINTING A TEST PAGE 136

74 - ADDING A PRINTER 137

75 - REVISION 139

SECTION 9 NETWORK CONCEPTS **140**

76 - NETWORKS 141

77 - THE INTERNET 142

78 - CONNECTING TO THE INTERNET 143

79 - CHOOSING AN ISP 144

80 - WI-FI NETWORKS 146

81 - COMMUNICATING ONLINE 148

82 - REVISION 150

SECTION 10 HEALTH AND SAFETY **151**

83 - SAFE AND PROPER PRACTICE 152

84 - PASSWORDS 153

85 - COMPUTER VIRUSES 154

86 - ANTIVIRUS SOFTWARE 155

87 - ACCESSIBILITY 157

88 - GREEN COMPUTING 158

89 - ROUTINE IT PROBLEMS 160

90 - COMPUTER MAINTENANCE 162

91 - CLEANING YOUR COMPUTER 164

92 - REVISION 165

ANSWERS **166**

RECORD OF ACHIEVEMENT MATRIX **169**

Section 1
Basics of ICT

By the end of this section you should be able to:

Understand the term ICT

Recognise the differences between hardware and software

Use different input, output and storage devices

Know how to connect peripheral devices

Appreciate the factors affecting device performance

Spot important health and safety issues when using ICT

Select the right software program(s) to complete a task

Work accurately, safely and securely

Work through the **Driving Lessons** in this section to gain an understanding of the above features.

For each **Driving Lesson**, read all of the **Park and Read** instructions and then, if applicable, perform the numbered steps of the **Manoeuvres**. Complete the **Revision** exercise(s) at the end of the section to test your knowledge.

BRIDGWATER COLLEGE LRC

Driving Lesson 1 - ICT Concepts

◲ Park and Read

The term **ICT** stands for **Information and Communication Technology**. Pretty much any device or computer program that creates, stores or uses digital information can be considered an ICT system, including:

- Hardware such as desktop computers, laptops, netbooks, tablets and games consoles.

- Software applications such as web browsers, word processors, spreadsheets, databases, e-mail systems, graphics programs and games.

- Internet technologies such as *Google*, *Twitter*, *Facebook* and *Flickr*.

- Mobile devices such as smart phones, GPS systems, media players, digital cameras, iPads and iPods.

- Peripheral items such as printers, scanners, keyboards and mice.

ⅈ *You will learn more about hardware, software, peripheral devices and Internet technologies later in this guide.*

Computing and mobile technologies have completely transformed how people live their lives – at home, in education and at work. It has changed how people communicate with each other, how they store and access information, how they work, and how they spend their spare time. In fact, ICT systems allow people to better explore ideas, handle lots of information, find answers to questions, solve problems, and become more productive in their personal and professional lives.

If you want to be an active member of your own society and succeed in education and a future career, your ability to fully understand and use ICT technology safely and effectively will be an essential skill.

ⅈ *ICT systems are used in more places than you may realise: car engines, vending machines, home heating systems. Even some "smart" refrigerators have built-in Internet connections to automatically reorder groceries.*

⌒ Manoeuvres

1. Does the term ICT just refer to computers such as desktop, laptop and tablet PCs?

2. Consider all of the ICT devices that you own or Internet services that you use. You will be surprised how many different types of technology you interact with on a daily basis.

Driving Lesson 2 - Using ICT Safely

▣ Park and Read

Before you start working with equipment of any kind, you first need to know how to use it safely and responsibly. ICT devices are no different, and whether you use them at home, in education, or as part of your job, you are required by law to take reasonable care of your own safety and the safety of others.

 In both education and work, the people in charge of you are legally required to make sure you are well-protected and well-trained. For ICT users, this means providing you with equipment that is safe, secure and comfortable to use.

Modern ICT systems present a number of health and safety hazards that you must be aware of. Whenever you use an electronic device of any sort, no matter where it is, you should always watch out for the following hazards:

- Electrical injuries and fires from damaged wires or incorrect connections

- Electrical injuries and fires from overloaded power sockets (too many plugs connected to one outlet)

- Injuries and fires caused by badly stored materials (paper and other items piled up and around equipment)

- Breakdowns and breathing problems due to poor ventilation (many ICT devices need to be kept cool and some types of printer can produce unhealthy fumes)

- Trips due to trailing cables or problems accessing your work area

- Injuries caused by incorrect equipment handling (heavy or large devices)

When you use ICT on the move you need to be even more alert for dangers. For example, watch out for any hazards that could trip you up or cause a serious fall, and never use a mobile device (such as a telephone or tablet computer) when driving or operating dangerous machinery.

 Never eat or drink when using an ICT device. Food and liquids can easily be dropped or spilled which can damage equipment or cause electrical injuries.

Driving Lesson 2 - Continued

Depending on your age, level of ability and where you study or work, there may also be other health and safety hazards to be aware of. For example, you may need to wear protective clothing and keep out of areas where dangerous materials or machinery are stored. Watch for warning signs and follow any health and safety information given to you.

 Always tell someone in charge about any health and safety concerns you have. If you do hurt yourself or damage a piece of equipment, you must report it.

Manoeuvres

1.   Look around you. Check that there are no cables lying across the floor that you or somebody else could trip over.

2.   Check that there are no cables hanging down behind your desk that could tangle with your feet as you work. This includes power cables and Internet connection wires.

 Take care when adjusting cables. Always make sure your computer equipment is turned off and unplugged from the wall before you start.

3.   Look out for and immediately replace worn or frayed cables. Never examine a suspect wire or device until it has been turned off and unplugged.

4.   Check for sockets or power extensions that have too many plugs in them. Overloaded electrical sockets can easily cause fires or injury.

5.   Remove any unnecessary clutter from your work environment and avoid storing items where they could fall and cause injury or damage.

6.   Finally, check your surroundings for any other dangers, obstructions, trip hazards (e.g. wires, boxes, bins and bags), fire hazards, and so on.

 In every building in which you study or work, you should always know where the emergency exits and fire extinguishers are located.

Driving Lesson 3 - Your Workspace

▣ Park and Read

If you sit at a computer or use ICT equipment for long periods of time, it can start to get uncomfortable and – in severe cases – cause injury. To stay safe and well you need to learn how to avoid these problems *before* they start. Remember: prevention is always better than cure!

When using ICT equipment always remember the following simple precautions:

- Take regular breaks away from all of your ICT devices (one or two minutes every hour).

- Look away from screens regularly (and remember to blink often).

- Vary your work activities so that you do not perform the same task for too long.

- Do not sit with a poor posture or hold heavy ICT devices for long periods of time.

- Use simple stretching exercises to relax your muscles and stay active.

If you use a desktop or laptop computer for any length of time, it is also important that you set up your work space correctly. The following advice will help:

- Position your computer monitor directly in front of you with the top of the screen at roughly the same height as your eyes.

- Adjust the position of your chair so that you can sit upright at your desk about one arm's length away from your screen (50 to 80 centimetres is recommended).

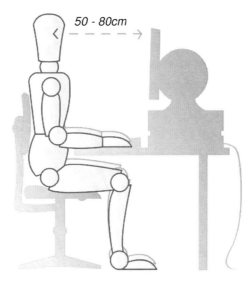

- Adjust the screen to reduce glare and reflections from lights or windows.

Driving Lesson 3 - Continued

- Set up your chair so that it fully supports your back and make sure your feet rest firmly on the floor. Foot and wrist rests can be used to help.

- Place your keyboard and mouse directly in front of you and do not stretch to reach them. Your forearms and hands should always remain parallel with the floor.

Manoeuvres

1. Adjust your chair so that your back is straight and your hands are placed comfortably over the mouse and keyboard. Your feet should lie flat on the ground

2. Check that the computer screen you are using is positioned at a comfortable height and angle so that you can see it without straining.

3. Make sure there is no glare or reflection from other light sources (i.e. windows or ceiling lights).

4. Adjust the position of the screen, keyboard and mouse so that you are comfortable operating the computer.

Driving Lesson 4 - Computing Hardware

▣ Park and Read

ICT devices come in a variety of forms: digital cameras, smart phones, MP3 players, and desktop, laptop and tablet computers. All of these devices are known as **hardware**, which is a term that refers to any piece of physical technology that you can touch.

Desktop PC including separate monitor, keyboard and mouse

Laptop

Tablet

Mobile Phone

Two of the most popular types of personal computing (**PC**) device are the **desktop computer** and the **laptop computer**. Smaller, cheaper versions of laptops known as **netbooks** are also quite common, but these simply allow users to connect to the Internet and often suffer from poor performance. Gaining in popularity are **tablet computers** which are smaller again and usually feature a touch screen. Of course, one of the most popular ICT devices in the world today is the **mobile phone**.

Hardware	Advantages	Disadvantages
Desktop PC	High performance; easy to upgrade and repair; lots of peripherals to attach; large monitor sizes	Large and can't be moved easily; requires a lot of dedicated desk space
Laptop PC	High performance; easy to move and use "on the go"; wireless network access	Usually more expensive than a desktop; higher chance of being lost, stolen or damaged; harder to upgrade and repair; short battery life; often causes poor posture
Netbook	Cheap, small, light and portable; wireless network access	Chance of being lost, stolen or damaged; low performance; hard to upgrade and repair; short battery life; causes poor posture

Driving Lesson 4 - Continued

Tablet	Very light and portable; easy to use; wireless network access	Slower than a laptop; almost impossible to upgrade; small screen and lack of features reduce productivity; short battery life
Mobile Phone	Very light and portable; **smart phones** have lots of communication features; 3G and 4G network access	Easy to lose; small screen size limits usefulness; very short battery life

Nearly all ICT computing devices share two important internal hardware components that work closely together: a **processor** and **memory**. The processor is the "brains" of a device and performs all of the basic calculations and functions that make it work. The memory is used to *temporarily* store programs of instructions and "active" data as they are being worked on by the processor.

 *A processor is also known as a **CPU (Central Processing Unit)**. It is a small microchip that can get very hot when in use and needs to be cooled (usually by a device's built-in fan).*

A device's memory is often referred to as **Random Access Memory (RAM)**. Unlike other ICT storage devices that take a small amount of time to read and write data, RAM memory can be accessed almost immediately. This allows the processor to step through instructions, access data and store the results of calculations very quickly.

 *Many ICT devices have built-in "**boot**" instructions stored on special **Read Only Memory (ROM)** chips. These are used to start the device and begin loading its operating system software (which you will learn more about in a later section).*

To be stored long-term, data needs to be recorded on a permanent storage device such as a hard disk drive. You will learn more about storage devices later in this section.

 It is important to realise that memory is <u>not</u> the same as storage. A device's memory temporarily holds data as the processor works on it; a storage device stores it permanently (or at least until it is manually deleted).

Finally, most computing devices feature one or more **optical disc drives** for reading from and writing to CD and DVD discs. These drives typically eject a tray into which a disc is placed; when the tray is closed the device will automatically recognise the new media and open it.

Driving Lesson 5 - Input and Output Devices

▣ Park and Read

Any piece of hardware that is used to enter information <u>into</u> an ICT system is known as an **input device**. There are many different kinds of input device available, some of which you will already be familiar with:

- Common computer peripherals such as keyboards, mice and trackballs

- Built-in control devices such as laptop touchpads or mobile phone touchscreens

- Gadgets for recording audio and video such as microphones and webcams

- Image capture devices such as scanners, photocopiers and digital cameras

- Barcode scanners, card readers and device docking stations

- Remote control devices such as wireless and TV games controllers

- Sensors that can detect changes in environmental conditions such as increased or decreased light, sound, temperature, pressure and movement.

ℹ️ *Sensors are often used in computer-controlled heating and air-conditioning systems to monitor and maintain building temperatures. Automatic security alarms and fire detection systems also use a combination of sensor inputs.*

Any piece of hardware that is used to send information <u>out</u> of an ICT system is known as an **output device**. Again, there are many different kinds of output device, including:

- Computer monitors and laptop, tablet, TV and mobile phone screens

- Projectors, media players and large video displays

- Speakers and headphones

- Computer-controlled motors, manufacturing machinery and industrial robots

- Printers and plotters (a plotter is a special high-quality printer that produces precise, large scale drawings such as building plans and engineering designs).

ℹ️ *The two most common types of printer are inkjet and laser. Inkjets are cheap to buy and are great for personal home use. Laser printers are usually more expensive but produce faster, higher quality prints that are ideal for use in business.*

Driving Lesson 6 - Connecting Peripherals

▣ Park and Read

Connecting peripherals such as printers, scanners, keyboards, mice, external disk drives and digital cameras to ICT devices is usually a simple case of "**plug and play**". Your ICT device will immediately notice that a peripheral has been connected and will automatically "install" (i.e. copy to your computer) the software needed to use it (known as a **driver**).

As you might expect, there are many ways you can connect a peripheral to your ICT device. The most popular is to use a **USB** cable (known as a **wired** connection). To do this, simply connect one end of the cable to your peripheral and the other to an empty USB **port** (socket) on your device. To help identify the right port, look for the USB icon shown below.

ℹ️ *Always follow the manufacturer's instructions when connecting a new peripheral.*

ℹ️ *USB connections are a very popular way to attach peripheral devices such as keyboards, mice, digital cameras and media players to a computer. Most modern computers have a number of USB ports available in easy-to-access locations.*

You can also use **Wi-Fi** or **Bluetooth** to connect a peripheral and ICT device together using radio waves (known as a **wireless** connection). One device transmits data and the other receives, similar to how TV and radio work. These are slightly more complicated to set up but allow you to place and use peripherals wherever you want without the need for connecting wires.

Driving Lesson 6 - Continued

i *Wireless connections are also ideal for connecting two ICT devices together and exchanging files between them.*

Many modern ICT devices also feature a variety of different port types, from power input sockets to video-output connectors. **Ethernet** ports for network connections and sockets for microphones and headphones are very common, as are slots for memory cards. Popular on laptop and tablet computers, **HDMI** ports can also be used to output a device's screen content to another device such as a TV (using an HDMI cable).

i *When purchasing a new peripheral, always ensure that your primary device supports the connection method required (i.e. it has the right types of port for the peripheral).*

i *You should never simply unplug an external storage device when you are finished using it. This could damage the files contained. Instead, you need to* **Eject** *the device properly. Instructions for doing this are given in Section 6.*

Driving Lesson 7 - Data Storage

⏻ Park and Read

All of the information that you enter into or use on an ICT device is known as data. It is usually held in a permanent storage area on your device and is moved into memory when required.

🛈 *Data held in memory will be lost when a computing device is switched off. To keep this data you must save it as a **file** on an available storage device.*

Data can be stored on your ICT device in many different ways depending on the type of technology you are using. For example, on a desktop or laptop computer, data can be saved to the **hard disk drive** (HDD) or **solid state drive** (SSD) inside of the device. On a mobile phone, MP3 player, digital camera or tablet computer, it can be stored on a **flash memory card**.

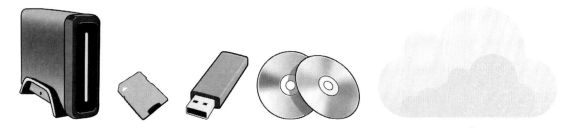

🛈 *A hard disk drive contains a spinning, magnetic disk for recording data (you can often hear it clicking and whirring inside your computer). Modern solid state drives have no moving parts, making them faster, quieter and more reliable.*

🛈 *"Flash" is used to describe memory that can be quickly deleted or saved.*

There are many other types of removable storage media available that allow you to store data or copy and move it between ICT devices. For example, you can store information on a recordable **CD** (compact disc) or **DVD** (digital versatile disc), an external **mobile hard drive**, an old-fashioned tape, or a more modern memory card or **USB memory stick**. As you will learn in the next section, these devices are great for allowing you to back-up your data.

🛈 *Music, videos and programs are often stored and distributed on **read-only memory (ROM)** media such as **Blu-ray**, CD and DVD discs. The data on these cannot be changed and no new data can be saved.*

🛈 *Some CDs and DVDs allow you to store, edit and delete the data stored on them. This facility requires compatible hardware and special discs that are available in two formats: **R** (Recordable) and **RW** (ReWriteable). CD-R and DVD-R discs can only have data saved to them once, whereas CD-RW and DVD-RW discs allow data to be saved and edited as many times as you like.*

Driving Lesson 7 - Continued

 If connected, you can also save or transfer files to another ICT device on a network. You can even store and share files in a private location on the Internet (often to a storage service in the cloud).

 The "cloud" is the name given to a range of online storage areas and Internet-based tools and services. Popular collaboration technologies such as Office 365 *and* GoogleDocs *operate in the cloud, allowing people to access, create, share and edit files from anywhere in the world using only their web-browser.*

The amount of information that you can store on a device is referred to as its **capacity**. Storage capacity uses several terms to describe the increasing amounts of data that can be recorded.

Capacity	Description
1 Bit (b)	The amount of storage space needed to hold either a 1 or a 0 in memory (**binary numbering**). This is the smallest unit of computer memory.
1 Byte (B)	Equal to 8 bits, this is the amount of storage space needed to hold one character (i.e. a single letter, number or symbol).
1 Kilobyte (KB)	1024 Bytes
1 Megabyte (MB)	1024 Kilobytes
1 Gigabyte (GB)	1024 Megabytes
1 Terabyte (TB)	1024 Gigabytes
1 Petabyte (PB)	1024 Terabytes

Storage devices range in size from small, low capacity memory cards through to high capacity hard disk drives. For example, a CD is able to store a maximum of 650MB of data, a DVD can store up to 4.5GB, a Blu-ray can store up to 50GB, and modern hard drives can store terabytes of information.

 Manoeuvres

1.   What is the smallest unit of computer memory?

2.   How many bits are there in a byte?

3.   How many kilobytes are there in a megabyte?

4.   How many megabytes are there in a gigabyte?

5.   How many kilobytes are there in a gigabyte?

Driving Lesson 8 - Computing Software

▣ Park and Read

The term **software** is used to describe a "**program**" of instructions that tells an ICT device what to do, how to do it, and when. Software is used to perform a specific task when "run" or "executed" on a device. Without software, most modern computing hardware wouldn't be much use at all.

The most important type of software is a device's **operating system**. This controls all of the hardware inside of the device, automatically manages memory and data storage, and provides the look, feel and functionality of the user-interface. It also allows you to organise files into folders, start other software, and manage the device's settings.

ⓘ Microsoft Windows *is the most popular type of computer and mobile device operating system. However, other types include* Linux, *Google's* Android, *and* Apple's iOS *and* MacOS.

ⓘ *Software packages that are used to perform a specific task, such as creating a document or accessing the Internet, are also known as* **applications** *("apps" on mobile devices). Application and program are often used interchangeably.*

Nearly all software programs obtained on CD/DVD or via a web download need to be **installed** on a compatible operating system before they can be used. As you will learn later, this is a simple, automatic process which copies all of the files needed to run the program to the correct location on the device. The program is then "registered" so it can be easily located and started.

ⓘ *The* Microsoft Office *application suite features a range of popular software programs for creating documents, spreadsheets, databases, presentations, publications and e-mails.*

In the course of your life, you will often find problems that can be solved using ICT. However, you need to be able to choose the best software program(s) for the task you have been given. To help you do this, the following notes will help you to understand the differences between the most popular types of office productivity software available.

Software Type	Description
Word Processing e.g. *Word*	Word processing software lets you create professional documents such as letters, essays, reports and books.
Spreadsheets e.g. *Excel*	Spreadsheet software allows you to work with lots of numbers and calculate a variety of different types of sums. It is often used to do accounts and budgets.

Presentations e.g. *PowerPoint*	Presentation software can be used to create slideshows to go with a spoken lecture or talk. It can also be used to create handouts for students, or automatic presentations that run in a loop.
Publications e.g. *Publisher*	Desktop publishing software can be used to create high quality printed materials with lots of graphics. This includes flyers, posters, banners, brochures, magazines, greeting cards and advertisements.
Databases e.g. *Access*	Databases can be used to store and manage large quantities of information (e.g. customer or product details). You can also query a database to find out information quickly.
Web Browsing e.g. *Internet Explorer*	Web browsing software allows you to access the vast amounts of information and file downloads available on the Internet.
E-mail e.g. *Outlook*	E-mail software allows you to send messages and file attachments to other ICT users anywhere in the world. You can also use this software to organise your time and create personal "to-do" lists and calendars.

 Microsoft's Internet Explorer *web browser is a very common application for accessing the Internet on a* Windows-*based device. However, other common web-browsing software includes* Google's Chrome, Mozilla's Firefox *and* Apple's Safari.

There are also many other, more specialised software applications available that can be used to help with a wide variety of tasks. Popular examples include:

- Photo and image editing software (e.g. *Adobe Photoshop*)
- Animation and multimedia software (e.g. *Adobe Flash*)
- 3D and computer-aided design (CAD) software (e.g. *Google Sketchup*)
- Audio and music editing software (e.g. *Audacity, Adobe Soundbooth*)
- Video editing software (e.g. *Windows Movie Maker, Adobe Premiere*)
- Web page design software (e.g. *Microsoft Expression Web, Adobe Dreamweaver*)
- Entertainment software (e.g. *BBC iPlayer, Apple iTunes*)
- Video games and mobile "apps" (e.g. *Google Maps, Yahoo Weather*)

 Not all software that you use is installed on your device. Web-based services such as Google, Facebook *and* Twitter *are installed on remote computers that can be located anywhere in the world. You will find out more about the latest Internet and communication technologies in section 9.*

Driving Lesson 9 - Software Licences

▣ Park and Read

All software products, from image editing programs and word processing applications to games and mobile apps, are the **copyright** property of the person or company that created them. When you buy (or download *free*) software, you get a **licence** to use a copy of it.

 *You do not own a program that you buy. You are simply granted a "software licence" to use it based on the terms of the **End-User Licence Agreement** (**EULA**). This is a legal contract between you and the owner of the software, and specifies exactly what you can and cannot do with the product.*

 Most end-user licence agreements appear when installing new software (or when signing up to a service online). You are required to read and agree to the terms of the agreement <u>before</u> using the software (even if it is free).

The EULA accompanying the software sets out exactly what you are permitted to do with it. This includes the number of times the software can be installed, the number of people who can use it, how it can be backed up, and a variety of other restrictions regarding transfer, leasing or renting of the product.

 Loaning or giving away copies of "proprietary" (i.e. non-free) software for others to use (or downloading pirate software to use yourself) is illegal. You can get into a lot of trouble doing this.

All software licences are different, but most fall into one of 5 distinct categories. These are described in the table below.

Licence Type	Description
Proprietary	A licence to use proprietary software must be paid for *before* you are allowed to use the program.
Trial	Trial software allows you to try out a program for a limited time (or with limited functionality). If you like it, you must pay for a licence to use the "full version".
Shareware	Shareware products can be given to others and trialled initially for free, but if you like and use it, you must pay for a licence.
Free Software	Sometimes referred to as "**freeware**", you can freely use and give away copies of free software to others.
Open Source	Open source software is the same as free software. However, the program's code is also available so programmers can make changes to the software.

Driving Lesson 10 - Device Performance

▣ Park and Read

The **performance** of an ICT device – how fast it is able to perform functions, process information and respond to user-input – is mainly based on the combination and speed of its hardware components. This includes:

- The speed of the CPU
- The amount of the RAM (memory)
- The capacity and speed of main storage devices
- The number of programs/processes running at once
- Network bandwidth

The relative importance of these factors will depend on the nature and number of tasks being performed. Any task involving thousands of complex calculations will depend heavily on CPU speed, whilst one involving huge quantities of data will be more affected by RAM size and storage device access times. Tasks involving network access will probably be restricted by connection bandwidth (i.e. the amount of data that can be transferred to and from the device).

ℹ️ *You will learn more about network bandwidth and Internet connection issues later in this guide.*

ℹ️ *The speed of a system is restricted by any component that causes a bottleneck in the flow of data. Generally speaking, a fast CPU combined with a small amount of RAM (or a slow CPU combined with a lot of RAM) will be limited by the slowest component.*

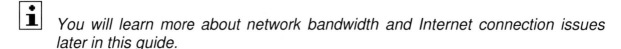

Although modern operating systems are designed to allow more than one program to run simultaneously, a large number of open programs and background processes will make enough demands on the CPU and RAM to produce a noticeable reduction in performance.

ℹ️ *Software, network bandwidth limitations and unwanted processes such as viruses can all negatively affect a device's performance. You will learn more about these later.*

An ICT device's screen is also an important consideration. Its size and **resolution** (i.e. the number of **pixels**, or individual dots of colour, that can be shown at once) are two important factors affecting its use. In general, the higher the resolution, the better the picture quality and the more information that can be displayed. However, small screens or high resolutions that try to cram too much information on-screen can negatively affect your ability to read text and interact with programs.

Driving Lesson 11 - Revision

▣ Park and Read

At the end of every section you get the chance to complete one or more revision exercises to develop your skills and prepare you for your ECDL certification test. You should aim to complete the following steps without referring back to the previous lessons.

↱ Manoeuvres

1.   What does the term ICT stand for?

2.   Give some examples of popular personal ICT computing devices.

3.   What does the term PC stand for?

4.   What do you understand by the term hardware?

5.   List the two main components of an ICT device that affect performance.

6.   What is RAM?

7.   Name some types of storage device.

8.   What do you understand by the term peripheral device?

9.   What do you understand by the term software?

10.   What is an operating system?

11.   Describe a good working environment relevant to desktop computer use.

12.   Describe some health and safety precautions which should be taken when working with computers.

 Sample answers can be found at the back of the guide.

 *Now complete the **Record of Achievement Matrix** at the back of the guide. You should only move on when confident with the topics and features described in this section.*

Section 2
Getting Started

By the end of this section you should be able to:

Start, restart and close down a device

Log on and log off Windows

Recognise and use the Desktop

Open, resize, reposition and close windows

Identify parts of a window

Understand the Start Menu and Taskbar

Start and close programs

Find help

Work through the **Driving Lessons** in this section to gain an understanding of the above features.

For each **Driving Lesson**, read all of the **Park and Read** instructions and then perform the numbered steps of the **Manoeuvres**. Complete the **Revision** exercise(s) at the end of the section to test your knowledge.

Driving Lesson 12 - Starting a Computer

▣ Park and Read

Although there are many different types of ICT hardware available, this guide focuses on the use of traditional computing devices such as desktops, laptops and tablet computers. To start such a device, it must be turned on using its main on/off power button.

ℹ️ *Before switching a computer on, briefly check for any lights – usually found on the front of the device – that show it is* already *activated. When left for a period of time, an ICT device may go into a dormant power-saving mode; either move the mouse or press a key on the keyboard to "wake it up".*

ꟼ Manoeuvres

1.   Locate your computer's power button. This is usually marked with the following symbol:

2.   If your computer is currently switched off (i.e. there are no lights on the front, the screen is blank and interacting with the mouse/keyboard has no effect) press the power button now. The computer starts.

3.   If you are using a separate monitor, this also needs to be turned on. If there are no lights on the front of the monitor and the screen is blank, locate and press its power button also.

ℹ️ *Computing devices go through a short start-up (or "**boot**") routine that detects all connected hardware and then loads the operating system.*

4.   After a moment the operating system is loaded. Please continue to the next lesson.

ℹ️ *This guide assumes that you are using* Windows 7.

Driving Lesson 13 - Logging On

▣ Park and Read

Windows allows more than one person to securely "sign in" and use a computer. Each person has their own settings and private storage spaces in which to keep their files.

To access your own files and start using the computer, you first need to **log on** to *Windows*. This involves entering a **username** and a **password** that is known only by you.

ℹ *Together, a username and password prove a person's identity and right to access files and shared devices. If a device is stolen or left unattended for a time, passwords will act as your own personal entry codes and stop unauthorised use.*

At home you may only need to select a username and, if required, enter a password. If your computer is connected to a network, however, you will first be prompted to log-on by pressing the key combination <**Ctrl Alt Del**>.

ℹ *You will need to press and hold the <**Ctrl**>, <**Alt**> and <**Delete**> keys down together.*

⤵ Manoeuvres

1. Depending on how your computer is set up, either select your username (if there is more than one user profile set-up) or press <**Ctrl Alt Del**> to begin the login process.

2. If your account is password protected, you will now be prompted to identify yourself. Enter your username (if not already selected) and then type your password. Press <**Enter**> to log on.

ℹ *Be careful not to forget a device's password. If you do it is very difficult to regain access to your profile and private storage spaces.*

3. After a moment the *Windows* **Desktop** is displayed. Please continue to the next lesson.

Driving Lesson 14 - The Windows Desktop

▣ Park and Read

When you have successfully logged on, the *Windows* **Desktop** will be displayed. This is the starting point for all tasks performed in *Windows*. From here it is possible to start all the programs installed on the computer and access all of the utilities and features of the operating system.

Icons

Desktop

Taskbar

Start Button

Notification Area

Show Desktop Button

 Windows can be customised according to your own preferences and that of the organisation which licenses it. Nearly every aspect of its appearance can be changed. For this reason, the screens shown in this guide may not quite match that of your computer. The basic layout and functionality, however, should be exactly the same.

The **Icons** that appear on the **Desktop** represent a small selection of the programs, folders and files stored on the computer. As you will learn later in this guide, they are small pictures that you usually "double click" to start or open. Most icons are accompanied by a short label to help you identify their use.

Computer   Recycle Bin   Internet

Along the bottom of the **Desktop** is an area known as the **Taskbar**. This is used to start, access and manage running programs and usually remains on screen at all times. As you will see later, the **Start** button – on the left of the **Taskbar** – is used to start nearly all programs and *Windows* features.

Driving Lesson 14 - Continued

More than one program can be run at the same time (this is known as **multi-tasking**), and as each program is started, it becomes active and a specific icon for it appears on the **Taskbar**. If the same program is opened many times, *Windows* may group icons together to save space.

i *The background of the currently active program icon is lighter than the others and appears with a border around it.*

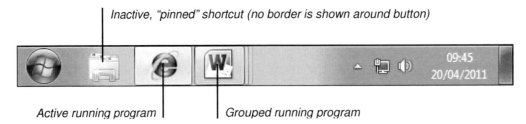

Inactive, "pinned" shortcut (no border is shown around button)

Active running program   *Grouped running program*

i *You can **Pin** your favourite programs to the **Taskbar** to make them easier to access. To do this, right click a program's icon and select **Pin to Taskbar**. Pinned items appear on the **Taskbar** but are not active until you click them.*

The **Notification Area** on the right of the **Taskbar** displays the date and time. On occasion, short status messages and alerts from *Windows* may also appear here. These are usually important and you should pay attention to them.

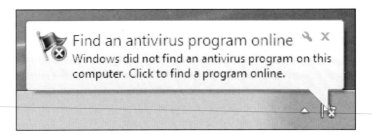

Some programs also install small icons in the **Notification Area** to provide status updates and allow you to quickly access settings (which you can do by "double-clicking" them, i.e. quickly clicking the left mouse button twice).

i *The **Show Desktop** button found to the far right of the **Taskbar** can be used to "minimise" (or hide) all windows and display the **Desktop**.*

Manoeuvres

1. Examine your own **Desktop** and identify all of the features described above. You will learn more about these features in the following lessons.

2. In particular, locate the **Recycle Bin**, the **Taskbar**, the **Start** button, the **Notification Area** and the **Show Desktop** button.

Driving Lesson 15 - The Start Menu

▣ Park and Read

At the left of the **Taskbar** is the **Start** button. Clicking the **Start** button opens the **Start Menu** which can be used to "run" any program installed on your computer. The **Start Menu** can also be used to search for information, access private files and folders, find help and support, and control your computer's settings.

⬑ Manoeuvres

1. From the *Windows* **Desktop**, click the **Start** button. The **Start Menu** appears.

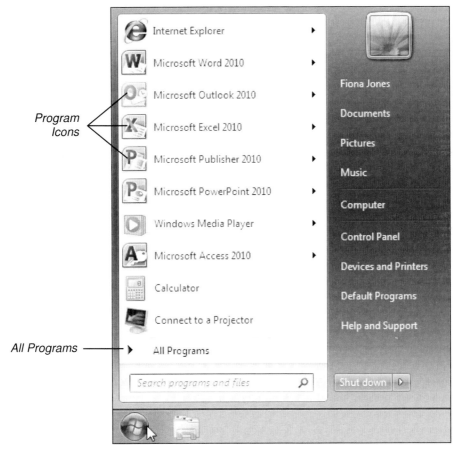

ℹ️ *A list of commonly used programs appears on the left of the **Start Menu**. These programs can be started by simply clicking them once. All programs (and often the files they create) have distinctive and representative icons to help you identify them at a glance. Observe the various icons that appear as you progress through this guide.*

2. Notice the buttons on the right of the **Start Menu**. These provide fast access to your private files and folders and allow you to access computer settings and find additional help and support.

Driving Lesson 15 - Continued

3.   Without clicking, locate and familiarise yourself with the following buttons. Some of these will be used later in this guide.

Documents	a private document storage location
Pictures	a private picture storage location
Music	a private music storage location
Computer	gives access to hardware and peripherals connected to your computer
Control Panel	allows control over your computer's settings
Devices and Printers	lets you to view, add, manage or remove peripheral devices and printers
Default Programs	allows you to choose the programs that *Windows* uses by default for specific tasks
Help and Support	gives access to the *Windows* help system

ℹ️ *As you will learn later, the **Shut down** button can be used to turn off or restart your computer. If there are any updates for your computer, these can be installed before shutting down.*

4.   Click **All Programs** towards the bottom of the left area of the **Start Menu**. A list containing all of the programs installed on your computer is shown.

ℹ️ *As you will see later, programs can be started by clicking their icon <u>once</u>.*

5.   Some programs are grouped into folders. Click on the **Accessories** folder once to **expand** it and display the contents.

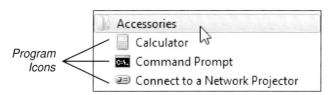

Program Icons

6.   Next, click on the **System Tools** folder to expand it.

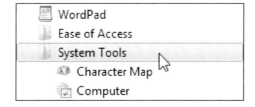

7.   Click the **Start** button again to close the **Start Menu**. Alternatively, simply click away from the **Start Menu** to close it.

Driving Lesson 16 - Window Layout

▣ Park and Read

Windows are rectangular boxes that appear on the **Desktop** and can be dragged around to any position and size you like. Inside a window, you can interact with programs, adjust computer settings, and manage files and folders. Many windows can be open at the same time and each can perform a variety of different, simultaneous tasks.

⌒ Manoeuvres

1. Click the **Start** button and then click **Computer** from the right of the **Start Menu**.

2. The **Computer** view is opened in a window. This view shows any and all storage devices that are currently connected to your computer (you may see a different set of icons).

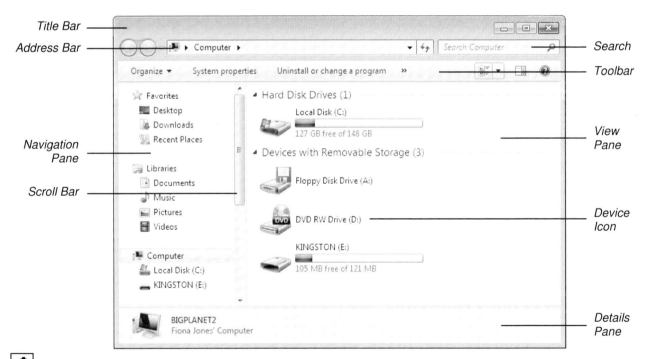

ℹ️ *This type of window is known as a **Windows Explorer** window. It allows you to navigate through the storage devices and folders on your computer. The **Address Bar** shows the current folder name that is on view in the window.*

ℹ️ *If your window does not appear with the **Navigation Pane** and **Details Pane** as shown above, click the **Organize** button on the **Toolbar** and select **Layout**. Make sure **Details Pane** and **Navigation Pane** are selected.*

Driving Lesson 16 - Continued

i *The **Title Bar** can be used to drag a window to another location. For windows containing programs/applications – which you will learn more about in the next section – it is also used to show the name of the program.*

3.   Locate the **Toolbar**. This is a row of buttons that allow you to perform simple tasks such as creating new folders or changing the current view.

4.   Notice the **Navigation Pane** on the left of the window. This can be used to explore the folder structure of your computer. The contents of the selected folder will appear in the **View Pane**.

5.   Brief information about any selected files, folders, devices and settings is shown in the **Details Pane**. Select one of the storage device icons shown on the **View Pane** (e.g. **Local Disk (C:)**) to find out more about it.

6.   Find the **Search** box to the right of the **Address Bar**. This feature allows you to search for files and folders stored on your device.

7.   Finally, whenever a window's contents are too big to view in one go, **scrollbars** are used. A vertical scrollbar allows you to move your view of the window's contents up and down; a horizontal scrollbar allows for side-to-side scrolling.

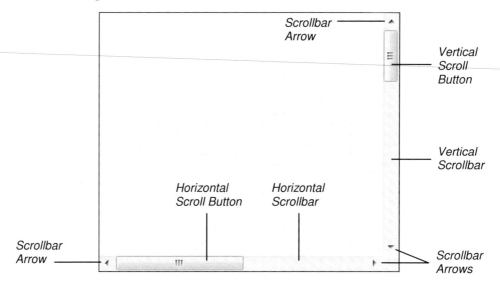

i *The position and size of the scroll buttons on a scrollbar indicate the relative view currently displayed in the window. The window's view can be moved by clicking the scrollbar arrows or by dragging the scroll button.*

i *You will learn more about all of the features described above as you progress through this guide.*

Driving Lesson 17 - Working with Windows

▣ Park and Read

Once opened, a window can be **maximised** (filling the whole screen), **minimised** (appearing only as an active button on the **Taskbar**), or **restored** (to any size in-between). If a window is *not* maximised, the size and position of it can also be changed.

⟰ Manoeuvres

1. Notice the three **Window Control Buttons** at the top right of the **Computer** window's **Title Bar**: **Minimize**, ⬜, **Maximize**, ⬜, and **Close**, ⬛.

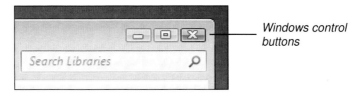

Windows control buttons

2. The **Maximize** button increases the size of the window to the maximum size available. If the **Computer** window is not maximised already, click the **Maximize** button now.

 If the window is maximised, the ***Maximize*** *button is replaced by the* ***Restore Down*** *button,* ⬚. *This restores the window to its last (non-maximised) size.*

3. Notice that the window now fills the screen. Click the **Restore Down** button, ⬚, to reduce the size of the window.

4. The **Minimize** button hides a window completely, leaving only its active button on the **Taskbar**. Click the **Minimize** button, ⬜, on the **Computer** window now.

5. When a window is minimised, the program or task inside the window continues to run. The **Computer** window can be restored by clicking its **Taskbar** button. Do that now.

6. Move the mouse pointer over the **Title Bar** of the **Computer** window. Click and drag the window to a new location anywhere else on the screen.

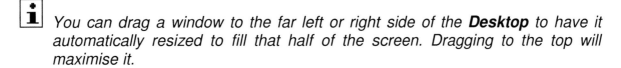 *You can drag a window to the far left or right side of the* ***Desktop*** *to have it automatically resized to fill that half of the screen. Dragging to the top will maximise it.*

Driving Lesson 17 - Continued

7.   The size of the window can also be changed. Move the mouse pointer over the right edge of the window until the pointer changes to a double headed arrow.

8.   Click and drag to increase or decrease the width of the window. The same technique can be used to increase or decrease the size of the window in all four directions.

9.   The size of a window can be changed in two directions at once. Place the mouse pointer over the bottom left or right corner of the window so that it changes to a two headed diagonal arrow.

10. Click and drag to increase or decrease the size of the window.

i *If more than one window is open at a time, they will overlap. The active window will always appear on top.*

11. Click the **Start** button and then click **Documents** from the right of the **Start Menu**. A second window is opened that shows your private documents. Drag the **Documents** window so that it appears on top of the **Computer** window (if it is not already).

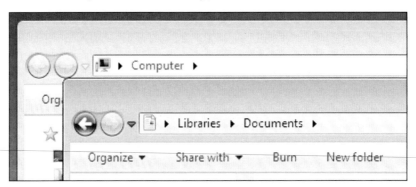

12. Notice that the **Taskbar** has automatically "grouped" the two **Windows Explorer** windows. Click the **Taskbar** button and a pop-up appears above allowing you to select which window you would like to activate.

13. Select **Computer** to activate that window and bring it to the front. Click anywhere on the **Documents** window behind to bring it to the top again.

i *You can also move between active windows by holding down <**Alt**> and pressing <**Tab**>.*

Driving Lesson 18 - Closing Windows

▣ Park and Read

The **Close** button, 🔳, found towards the top right of every window, closes that window. Any processes running *within* it are also stopped. For example, when running a program, closing its window will also end the program.

⌐ Manoeuvres

1. Click the **Close** button, 🔳, in the top right of the **Documents** window. The window is closed.

ⓘ *Notice that the **Documents** icon on the **Taskbar** is no longer active.*

2. Similarly, close the **Computer** window leaving only your **Desktop** on-screen.

ⓘ *Windows can also be closed by right clicking their buttons on the **Taskbar** and selecting **Close window**.*

ⓘ *The keyboard shortcut <**Alt F4**> will also close the currently active window.*

Driving Lesson 19 - Starting Programs

🄿 Park and Read

All programs available in *Windows* can be run using the **Start** button on the **Taskbar**. Some simple utility programs such as a *Calculator* and *Notepad* are provided with *Windows*. However, more complex and powerful software such as *Microsoft Office* needs to be purchased separately and installed from CD/DVD or via a web download (which you will learn more about later).

⟳ Manoeuvres

1. Click the **Start** button once and then select **All Programs** to display a list of all of the programs that are currently installed on your computer.

2. Click the **Accessories** folder once to open it, and then click once on **Calculator** to start the *Calculator* program. The **Start Menu** closes automatically.

3. The *Calculator* program runs and appears in its own window. This useful tool is ideal for performing simple calculations – try it.

4. Click the **Minimize** button, . The program is minimised and appears as a button on the **Taskbar**. Although not visible, the program is still running in the background.

5. Use the **Start Menu** to run a second instance of the *Calculator* program. There are now two *Calculators* running (which can be used completely independently). Notice that *Windows* automatically groups the **Taskbar** buttons.

Driving Lesson 19 - Continued

6. From the **Accessories** folder in the **Start Menu**, run the *Notepad* program. This useful tool allows you to create and work with basic text files – give it a try.

> **i** *Programs are traditionally known as* **executable** *files. When you run a program, you are said to execute it.*

7. From the **Accessories** folder, run the *WordPad* program. This tool also allows you to create and work with text but offers more font formatting, graphics and presentation features – give it a try.

> **i** *You will learn how to use more of* WordPad's *features in Section 4.*

8. When you are finished, click the *WordPad* program's **Close** button, [×]. If you are prompted to save any changes that you have made, select **Don't Save**. The program is closed and is no longer running.

9. Close *Notepad* without saving any changes.

10. Close both instances of the *Calculator* program (including the minimised one).

11. Next, explore some of the other programs installed on your computer by yourself. Don't be afraid to experiment and run programs that are available on the **Start Menu** – this is perfectly safe and will never cause any damage to your computer.

> **i** *Why not try the fun* Paint *program (found in* **Accessories**) *or the useful* Windows Media Player *that can be used to create and view your own music and video libraries?*

12. *Microsoft Office* is a collection of very powerful computer programs that are used by businesses and individuals around the world. Installed on most *Windows* computers, the package contains a number of well known programs such as *Word, Excel, PowerPoint, Publisher, Access* and *Outlook*. Can you find and start these on your computer?

13. When you are finished, close any open programs and return to the **Desktop**.

> **i** *Some programs such as antivirus utilities will run automatically when you turn your computer on. Others can be started as and when needed.*

> **i** *Icons for programs can be placed on the* **Desktop**. *Double-click those icons to run the program. If an icon for a program is available on the* **Taskbar***, you simply need to single-click it.*

Driving Lesson 20 - Unresponsive Programs

◨ Park and Read

Every once in a while a program will stop working when you are using it, often with little or no warning. In this case the program is said to have **crashed**. Fortunately, this does not happen very often, but when it does it is very easy to close and then restart the program.

i *Saving your work regularly will help avoid data loss as a result of program crashes.*

⬑ Manoeuvres

1. Using the **Start Menu**, start the *Calculator* program.

2. Assume this program has crashed and stopped working. When this happens the program will no longer respond to mouse clicks and key presses. In many cases you will not be able to use the **Close** button to end the program.

3. To force the program to close, press the key combination <**Ctrl Alt Del**>.

4. From the options that appear, select **Start Task Manager**. The **Windows Task Manager** dialog box appears.

5. Display the **Applications** tab to find the *Calculator* program running (other programs may appear here also).

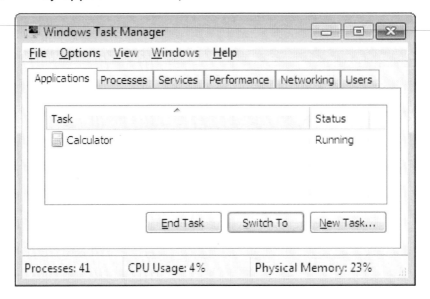

6. Select **Calculator** from the list and click **End Task**. The *Calculator* program is closed immediately.

7. Close the **Windows Task Manager** to return to the **Desktop**.

Driving Lesson 21 - Finding Help

⊞ Park and Read

Windows has a built-in **Help** facility to assist you when you have problems using your computer.

⬏ Manoeuvres

1. Click the **Start** button and then select **Help and Support**. The **Windows Help and Support** window appears.

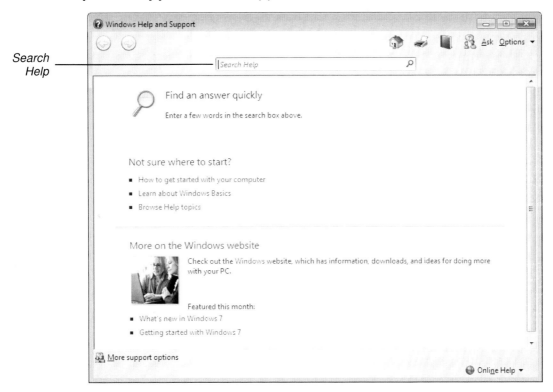

2. Examine the content of the window. Notice that help can be found by typing keywords into the **Search Help** box or by following on-screen links.

3. Click on one of the links (e.g. "**Learn about Windows Basics**", if present). This displays a page containing more detail about the selected topic, with more links to further detailed information.

4. Explore the help content by following links. The **Back** button, 🔙, can be used to return to a previous page.

ℹ️ The **Home** button, 🏠, can be used to return to the starting help page.

ℹ️ To obtain a printed copy of a page, click the **Print** button, 🖨️. You will learn more about printing later in this guide.

Driving Lesson 21 - Continued

5.   Next, click the **Browse Help** button, , if it is not already selected. This displays general help for *Windows* arranged like chapters in a book.

6.   Click one of the links shown and then follow some of the topics to explore the help content in more detail.

*A quick method of locating help is to use the **Search Help** box.*

7.   Type the keyword **printers** into the **Search Help** box and then click the **Search Help** button, (or press <**Enter**>).

8.   A list of topics matching the search is displayed. Locate and click a topic about installing a printer to find out more about how to do this.

Topics are usually shown in order of relevance with the best results at the top.

*If your computer is connected to the Internet, make sure that **Online Help** is selected in the bottom right corner of the **Windows Help and Support** window. This provides a wider range of up-to-date help content.*

9.   Using whichever technique you prefer, find a page of help on how to change your desktop background picture.

10.   Next, find out more about the following useful *Windows* utility programs: *Paint*, *WordPad* and *Calculator*.

11.   Finally, find help on how to shut down your computer. Discover why it is important to close down a computer properly.

12.   When you are finished, use the **Close** button, , to close the **Windows Help and Support** window.

*Many windows and dialog boxes can access relevant areas of the help system directly by means of a **Help** menu or **Help** button, .*

*Most programs/applications have their own internal **Help** systems with content that is relevant to their operation.*

Driving Lesson 22 - Logging Off

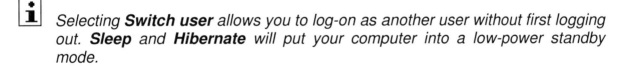 Park and Read

If you use a computer in a public place or you share your computer with others, you must always log off when you finish your work. This does not shut the computer down completely but simply ends your session and allows other people to log on afterwards.

Logging off closes any open windows or running programs. Importantly, anyone who tries to use the computer after you will not be able to gain access to your private files.

Manoeuvres

1.   Click the **Start** button to open the **Start Menu**.

2.   Then, click the arrow on the **Shut down** button (be careful not to click the **Shut down** button itself as this will turn off your computer).

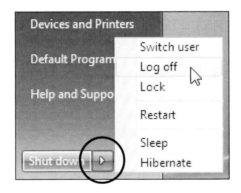

3.   From the options that appear, click **Log off**.

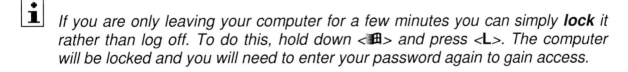 *Selecting **Switch user** allows you to log-on as another user without first logging out. **Sleep** and **Hibernate** will put your computer into a low-power standby mode.*

4.   You are now logged out of *Windows* and returned to the log-on screen. Log back in again.

*If you are only leaving your computer for a few minutes you can simply **lock** it rather than log off. To do this, hold down <▦> and press <**L**>. The computer will be locked and you will need to enter your password again to gain access.*

Driving Lesson 23 - Shutting Down Windows

▣ Park and Read

If *Windows* is **shut down** abnormally, perhaps if electricity is cut off or the battery removed, any unsaved data in open programs can be lost. In addition, operating system files can be damaged which may prevent *Windows* from working correctly. Shutting down your computer properly prevents these problems.

Shutting down *Windows* also turns a computer off. To start it up again, you will need to use the main on/off power button.

⤵ Manoeuvres

1. To shut down *Windows*, first click the **Start** button. Then, locate the **Shut down** button.

ℹ️ *If you are running any programs, it is always best to close these first before shutting down* Windows.

ℹ️ *If the* **Shut down** *button appears with a small shield icon,* 🛡️, *then updates to your operating system and software are ready to be installed. This will be done automatically as the computer shuts down.*

2. Click **Shut down**. After a few moments *Windows* will close and the computer will power-down. It is now turned off and is safe to disconnect from the power supply (if needed).

3. Start the computer and log-in again.

4. When the **Desktop** appears, display the **Start Menu**. This time, click the arrow on the **Shut down** button, ▷.

5. From the options that appear, select **Restart**. *Windows* and the computer both shut down but automatically restart again.

ℹ️ *Restarting a computer is often required when changes are made to* Windows' *settings or new programs are added or removed. In addition, if you experience problems with* Windows *programs or computing performance, try restarting – this can solve many problems.*

6. Log-in to *Windows* again and return to the **Desktop**.

Driving Lesson 24 - Revision

■ Park and Read

At the end of every section you get the chance to complete one or more revision exercises to develop your skills and prepare you for your ECDL certification test. You should aim to complete the following steps without referring back to the previous lessons.

⌐ Manoeuvres

1. Using the **Start Menu**, open the **Computer** window.

2. Single-click to select devices in the **View Pane** to find out more about them in the **Details Pane**.

3. **Maximize** the window, and then **Restore** it.

4. **Minimize** the window, and then **Restore** it (by clicking its button on the **Taskbar**).

5. Reduce the size of the window a little and then move it to the top right corner of the screen.

6. Dock the window on the right half of the screen. Hint: drag the window to the far right of the screen and then release.

7. Close the window.

8. Start the *Calculator* program. Using the utility, find out the result of multiplying **155** by **349**.

9. Close the *Calculator* program.

10. Use **Help** to find out more about customising the **Start Menu**.

11. Close the **Help** window.

12. Log-off *Windows* and then log back in again.

13. Restart your computer and then log back in again.

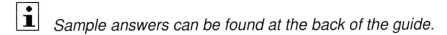

Sample answers can be found at the back of the guide.

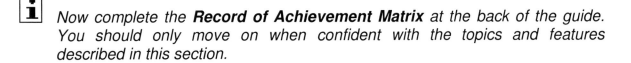

*Now complete the **Record of Achievement Matrix** at the back of the guide. You should only move on when confident with the topics and features described in this section.*

Section 3
Files and Folders

By the end of this section you should be able to:

Use Windows Explorer and folder views

Recognise common file types and icons

Select multiple files and folders

Create and organise folders

Copy, move and rename files and folders

Delete files and folders and use the Recycle Bin

Discover file and folder properties

Sort and search for files and folders

Work through the **Driving Lessons** in this section to gain an understanding of the above features.

For each **Driving Lesson**, read all of the **Park and Read** instructions and then perform the numbered steps of the **Manoeuvres**. Complete the **Revision** exercise(s) at the end of the section to test your knowledge.

Driving Lesson 25 - File and Folder Navigation

▣ Park and Read

A **file** is a small package of information that contains data. As you will learn later in this section, there are many different types of files, from documents and pictures to MP3 songs and even programs.

To store any type of file on a computer it must be placed in a **folder** (also known as a **directory**). This is simply a container that allows you to organise files into separate, logical groups.

Importantly, folders can contain an almost unlimited number of other folders – known as **subfolders**. In turn, these subfolders can contain more subfolders. This is known as a **hierarchical** file storage system.

ⓘ *Files that are related to one another, or belong in the same logical group as each other, should be stored together in the same folder. Subfolders within can be used to organise files into even more specific groups, making future file searches easier.*

In *Windows*, every storage device's folder structure is shown in the **Navigation Pane**, with the contents of a selected folder shown in the **View Pane**.

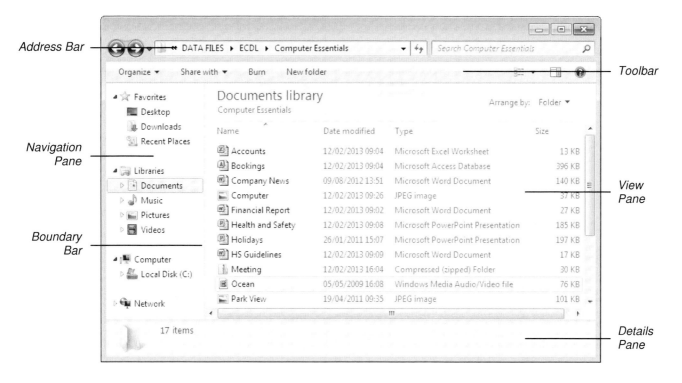

⌐ Manoeuvres

1. Open the **Start Menu** and then select **Documents**. This will open **Windows Explorer** and display the contents of the **Documents** library.

Driving Lesson 25 - Continued

i *In* Windows, *you may notice that your documents, music, pictures and videos appear in their own separate* **Libraries**. *These are simply the merged contents of one or more folders, and are designed to bring together files of similar types into one simple view.*

2. The data files for this guide have been placed in the **Documents** library. The folder **DATA FILES** will appear in the **View Pane**.

Folder Icon — DATA FILES

i *Notice the folder icon. Variations of this are always used to represent a folder. To open a folder, simply double-click it.*

3. Double-click the **DATA FILES** folder icon to open that folder and view its contents. Notice that the path in the **Address Bar** changes to show that you are now within the **DATA FILES** folder.

▸ Libraries ▸ Documents ▸ DATA FILES ▸

i *A* **path** *is the name given to the unique location of a file in a computer system. It describes the route you must take through the folders to find a file. Each folder in the path is usually separated by a ▸ or \ symbol.*

4. Locate the **Navigation Pane**. This can also be used to explore the folder structure of available storage devices more easily.

i *Other devices and network locations – if available – appear in the* **Navigation Pane**. *These can be selected and explored in exactly the same way as your local* **Documents** *folders.*

5. Move the mouse pointer over the **Navigation Pane** and small **Expand/Collapse** buttons appear to the left of the folder/device names.

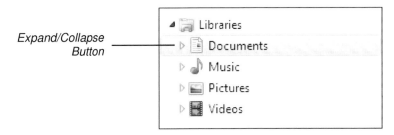

Expand/Collapse Button

Driving Lesson 25 - Continued

6. For example, notice that the **Documents** folder has an **Expand** button, 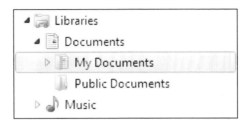, in front of it. This means that it contains one or more subfolders.

7. Click the **Expand** button for **Documents** once and observe the effect.

8. The folder is *expanded* and the subfolders contained within are displayed underneath. Notice that the **Expand** button has now changed to a **Collapse** button, 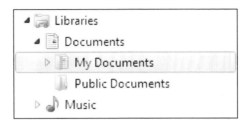.

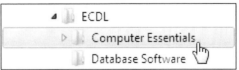

9. To hide the subfolders again, click the **Collapse** button next to **Documents**. The folder is *collapsed* and the subfolders within are hidden.

i *Depending on your computer, some folders may not appear exactly as described. You may need to substitute different folder names where appropriate.*

10. Next, expand the **Documents** folder again. Then, expand folders in the following order: **My Documents**, **DATA FILES**, **ECDL**. Data files for this (and possibly other) *ECDL* training guides are shown within, grouped by module name.

i *You can increase or decrease the space shared by the **Navigation Pane** and **View Pane** by dragging the **Boundary Bar** between them left or right.*

11. Click once on the **Computer Essentials** folder (not the **Expand/Collapse** buttons) to display the files contained in the **View Pane**. 18 items are displayed.

12. Locate the **Back** button, found to the left of the **Address Bar**. This moves the window's view backwards through all previously viewed folders (one step at a time). Click it <u>once</u>.

Back Button ——————   —————— Forward Button

13. Click the **Forward** button to return to the **Computer Essentials** folder.

i *Each of the folder names in the path on the **Address Bar** can also be clicked to return directly to that folder.*

Driving Lesson 26 - Folder Views

⊟ Park and Read

There are 8 **View Pane** folder views available in **Windows Explorer**. In practice you can use whichever you find most appropriate and useful. However, it is recommended that you use the default **Details** view for this guide.

⟨⟩ Manoeuvres

1.   On the **Toolbar**, locate the **Change your view** button, [icon]. ⎯⎯ *More options*

2.   Click the <u>drop-down arrow</u> on the button (labelled **More options**) and make sure that **Details** is selected. This default view shows file names listed in alphabetic order with file date, type and size information.

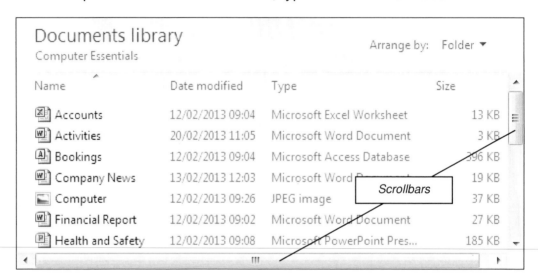

ℹ️   *If scrollbars appear on the right and bottom of the window then there is too much information to show in the space available. Click and drag these up/down or left/right to view more of the window's contents.*

3.   Click the **Change your view** button (not the **More options** drop-down arrow) to select the next view available (**Tiles**). Depending on the size of the **View Pane**, the files are displayed in a grid with large icons.

4.   Next, try changing the view to show folder contents as **Medium Icons**. Observe the effect: icons are shown from left to right with file names below. Try **Small Icons**, **Large Icons** and **Extra Large Icons**.

5.   Finally, change the view to **List**. Files are now shown in a multi-column list with small icons.

6.   Continue to click the **Change your view** button until you return to **Details** view (or use the **More options** drop-down arrow to go directly to it).

Driving Lesson 27 - File Types and Icons

P Park and Read

Nearly every file in *Windows* has a **file extension**; a short combination of letters that identifies a file's **type** (e.g. a *Word* document or *Excel* spreadsheet). These appear in the file's name after a full stop symbol. Although file extensions are normally hidden in **Windows Explorer**, it is still important that you learn how to recognise them. Some common file types are listed below.

Extension	File Type
docx/doc	*Microsoft Word* document
xlsx/xls	*Microsoft Excel* spreadsheet
pptx/ppt	*Microsoft PowerPoint* presentation
accdb/mdb	*Microsoft Access* database
pub	*Microsoft Publisher* publication
pdf	*Adobe's* portable document format
wma/mp3/wav	Audio files
mov/avi/mp4	Movie files
jpg/gif/png/bmp	Graphics or image files
txt	A plain text file
rtf	A text file with additional text formatting (rich text)
csv	A text file containing comma separated values
htm/html	General web page format
zip	A compressed file or folder (see lesson 57)
exe	An "executable" software program that will run (and perform a task in *Windows*) when double clicked

i *Image files come in a variety of different forms. The most popular are JPG files which are used to store photos captured by a digital camera or scanner. Other formats such as GIF or PNG are mostly used to store smaller, less-detailed graphics such as those that appear on web pages (i.e. buttons, logos, backgrounds, page design artwork, etc.).*

i *Many programs allow you to save your documents or images as a PDF. These are small, print-ready versions of a file that are easy to send via e-mail or download from the Internet. Importantly, a PDF file can be opened without needing the software that was used to create it.*

Driving Lesson 27 - Continued

When a new file is created using an application, the correct file extension is automatically added to it. You can then identify the file's type by the extension and icon displayed.

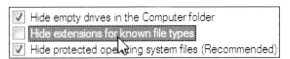 **Manoeuvres**

1. To view file extensions, click the **Organize** button on the **Toolbar** and select **Folder and search options**.

2. Display the **View** tab. From here you can adjust a number of settings which control how files and folders are displayed in *Windows*.

3. <u>Remove</u> the tick from **Hide extensions for known file types** (if it is not unchecked already).

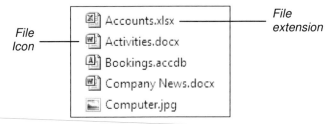

4. Click **OK** to apply the change and close the dialog box.

5. From the view of files in the **Computer Essentials** folder, identify each of the file types by their file extensions.

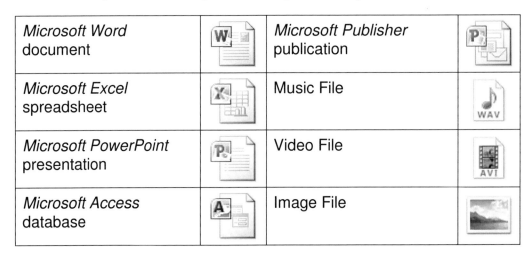

6. Notice the file **icons**. Most file types and programs have their own unique icons so that you can identify them at a glance. Popular file icons include:

Microsoft Word document		Microsoft Publisher publication	
Microsoft Excel spreadsheet		Music File	
Microsoft PowerPoint presentation		Video File	
Microsoft Access database		Image File	

i *If applicable, Windows will show a small thumbnail preview of a file's contents instead of a default icon. This is very common with image files.*

Driving Lesson 28 - Sorting Files and Folders

◨ Park and Read

The list of files shown in the **View Pane** can be sorted in different ways. For example, files can be sorted in ascending or descending alphabetical order or increasing or decreasing file size.

⬑ Manoeuvres

1. The **Computer Essentials** data files folder should currently be open with **Details** view selected. Examine the **Header Bar** that appears in this view.

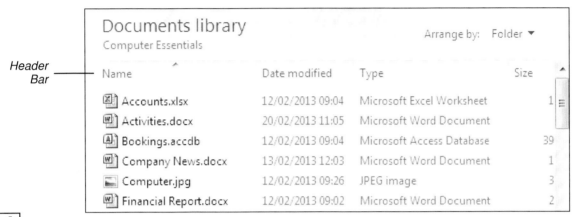

ⓘ *The **Details** view shows items in a table. Each row represents a different file or folder with multiple columns describing their **properties** (i.e. information about the file or folder). The **Header Bar** indicates the types of properties shown.*

ⓘ *By default, files and folders are sorted by name in ascending order. To show this, a small upwards arrow icon, ▲, appears by the property **Name**. Where folders and files appear together, folders are always grouped together first.*

2. The type of sort can be changed by clicking once on a relevant **Header Bar** property. Click once on **Name** to reverse the sort and show files in reverse alphabetical order. Notice that the arrow icon is reversed to indicate a *descending* sort.

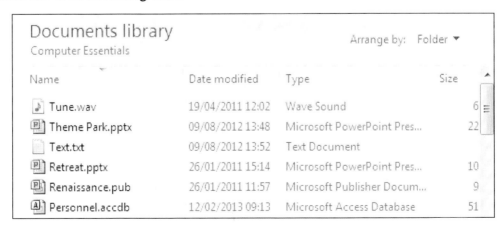

Driving Lesson 28 - Continued

3.   Click the **Date modified** property to sort files into order by date changed. This is useful for finding files that have been used recently.

4.   Click the **Date modified** property again to display files in reverse order.

5.   Click the **Type** property to sort the files by file type. This will group all similar files and is useful if you want to see and count all the files of one type, e.g. all the documents.

6.   Click the **Size** column heading to sort the list in order of size, largest first (descending). This is useful for finding the largest files in a folder. Click the heading again to display files in the reverse order (ascending).

i   *You can adjust column widths to show or hide the information shown.*

7.   Place your mouse pointer over the border between the **Name** and **Date modified** properties on the **Header Bar**. It changes to a double-headed arrow, ✛, as shown below.

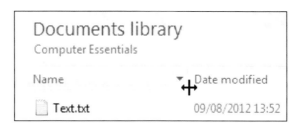

8.   Click and drag the border right a little to increase the width of the column. Then try clicking and dragging left to reduce the width of the column.

i   *You can double-click a property's border to automatically adjust the width to show all information in that column.*

9.   Place your mouse pointer over the border between the **Name** and **Date modified** properties again. When it changes to a double-headed arrow, ✛, double-click. The column's width is automatically adjusted.

10. Maximise the window if it is not already. Then, adjust the sizes of other property columns so that all information is fully displayed.

11. Finally, click the **Name** heading again to sort the files back into ascending alphabetical order.

i   *Additional file and folder properties can be added to **Details** view (e.g. file creation date, author name, keywords, etc.). To do this, right click the **Heading Bar** and select the property required.*

i   *Advanced sorting options can be accessed by clicking the drop-down arrow, ▾, that appears when the mouse pointer is placed over a **Header Bar** property.*

Driving Lesson 29 - Creating New Folders

⊞ Park and Read

You can create and use folders to sort and organise files into logical groups so that they are easier to find later. However, it is important that you use sensible and meaningful names to make it easy to see at a glance what a folder contains.

ℹ️ *It is always important to be well organised. If you don't keep a tidy file and folder system you will never be able to find anything when you need it.*

↱ Manoeuvres

1. On the **Toolbar**, click the **New folder** button, New folder , to create a new folder in the current location. A new folder appears and you are prompted to give it a name.

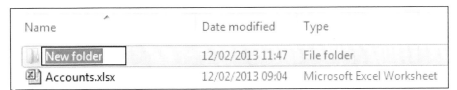

2. Type in the name **Reports** and press <**Enter**>. It appears at the top of the list in the **View Pane** (recall that all folders appear first, *before* files).

3. Using the same technique, create 4 more new folders called **Publications**, **Presentations**, **Image Library** and **Databases**.

4. Open the **Presentations** folder and then create two subfolders within called **Training** and **Marketing**.

ℹ️ *Files that are related to one another, or belong in the same logical group as each other, should be stored together in the same folder.*

5. To return to the previous folder, click the **Back** button located to the left of the **Address Bar**.

ℹ️ *A new folder can also be created by right-clicking and selecting **New | Folder**.*

Driving Lesson 30 - Selecting Items

▣ Park and Read

In the *Driving Lessons* that follow you will learn how to copy and move files and folders. However, before that, you first need to be able to **select** those files and folders. To do this, you simply need to click them once in the **Navigation** or **View Pane**.

ℹ *Single-click a file or folder to select it. Double-clicking will open them.*

To save time, it is often useful to be able to select multiple files and folders at once. There are a number of techniques for doing this.

⌐ Manoeuvres

1. With the **Documents** window open and the contents of the **Computer Essentials** data files folder on view, click once on the file **Financial Report**.

2. Notice that the file appears highlighted to indicate it is selected.

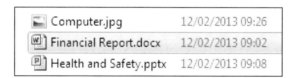

Computer.jpg	12/02/2013 09:26
Financial Report.docx	12/02/2013 09:02
Health and Safety.pptx	12/02/2013 09:08

3. Next, click once to select and highlight the file **Holidays**. Notice that **Financial Report** is no longer selected.

ℹ *To select more than one file at once, hold <**Ctrl**> and single-click each item.*

4. Select the file **Financial Report** again. Then, press and hold down <**Ctrl**> and click the **Holidays** file. Both are now selected.

| Financial Report.docx |
| Health and Safety.pptx |
| Holidays.pptx |

5. Holding down <**Ctrl**>, select the files **Ocean** and **Renaissance** also.

ℹ *You can select both files and folders at the same time using this technique.*

6. Holding down <**Ctrl**>, select the folders **Presentations** and **Publications**. Notice that "**6 items selected**" appears on the **Details Pane**.

7. Release <**Ctrl**> and click any file or folder to select just that item.

Driving Lesson 30 - Continued

8. Next, try selecting the items **Reports**, **Accounts**, **Computer** and **Theme Park** at the same time.

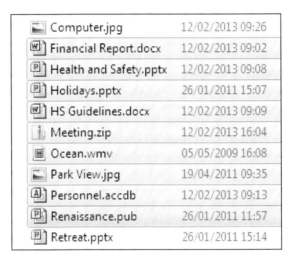 *To select a block of files or folders, hold <**Shift**> and click the first and last item in the range.*

9. Select the file **Financial Report** again by single-clicking it. Then, press and hold down <**Shift**> and click the **Renaissance** file. A continuous block of 9 items is now selected.

Computer.jpg	12/02/2013 09:26
Financial Report.docx	12/02/2013 09:02
Health and Safety.pptx	12/02/2013 09:08
Holidays.pptx	26/01/2011 15:07
HS Guidelines.docx	12/02/2013 09:09
Meeting.zip	12/02/2013 16:04
Ocean.wmv	05/05/2009 16:08
Park View.jpg	19/04/2011 09:35
Personnel.accdb	12/02/2013 09:13
Renaissance.pub	26/01/2011 11:57
Retreat.pptx	26/01/2011 15:14

10. Release <**Shift**> and click any file or folder to select just that item.

11. Next, try selecting the block of 15 items in the range between **Presentations** and **Park View**.

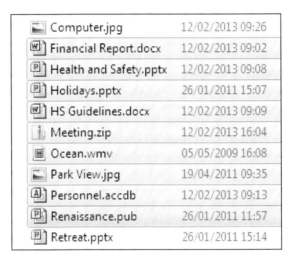 *To select all items in a folder press <**Ctrl A**>.*

12. Press <**Ctrl A**> to select all the files currently in the **View** window.

13. Finally, click any single file or folder to select just that item.

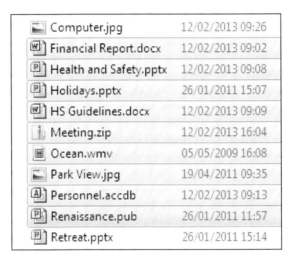 *All methods of selecting multiple files and folders work equally well in any view. Mixtures of files and folders can also be selected, copied or moved in the same operation.*

Driving Lesson 31 - Copying Files

▣ Park and Read

There are many reasons why you might want to create a copy of a file. For example, you may want to create a copy of your data for backup purposes, to place on an external storage device so that you can take it elsewhere, or to use as a starting point for new data.

⬈ Manoeuvres

1. The **Documents** window should still be open with the contents of the **Computer Essentials** data files folder on view. Select the file **Financial Report**.

2. From the **Toolbar**, click the **Organize** button and select **Copy**. The file is copied and placed in memory.

3. Click the **Organize** button again and select **Paste**. The copied file is pasted into the current folder.

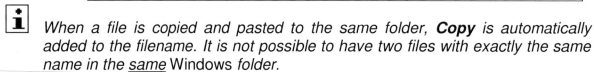

🖻 Computer.jpg	12/02/2013 09:26	JPEG image
📰 Financial Report - Copy.docx	12/02/2013 09:02	Microsoft Word Document
📰 Financial Report.docx	12/02/2013 09:02	Microsoft Word Document
📰 Health and Safety.pptx	12/02/2013 09:08	Microsoft PowerPoint Presentation

ⓘ *When a file is copied and pasted to the same folder, **Copy** is automatically added to the filename. It is not possible to have two files with exactly the same name in the <u>same</u> Windows folder.*

4. Create a new folder called **Copies**.

5. Select the file **Bookings** and, using the **Organize** button, make a copy.

6. Open the new **Copies** folder and, using the **Organize** button again, **Paste** the copied file.

ⓘ *Notice that the file retains the same filename (i.e. **Copy** is not added) as it was not pasted into the same folder as the original file.*

7. Click the **Back** button once to return to the **Computer Essentials** folder.

8. Select the file **Computer** by clicking it once. Whilst holding down the <**Ctrl**> key, drag the file over the **Copies** folder. Notice that the mouse pointer changes to the **Copy to** cursor.

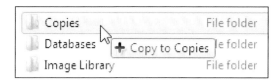

Driving Lesson 31 - Continued

9.   Release the mouse button to drop a copy of the file into the **Copies** folder, and then release the **<Ctrl>** key. Open the **Copies** folder to find the copied file.

i   *Changes made to a copied file will not affect the original.*

10.   Click the **Back** button once to return to the **Computer Essentials** folder.

i   *Files can also be copied using the **Navigation Pane**.*

11.   Expand the **Computer Essentials** folder in the **Navigation Pane** (if it is not already). The 6 folders created earlier appear underneath.

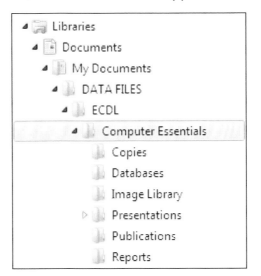

12.   Click once to select the file **Health and Safety** in the **View Pane**.

13.   Then, hold down **<Ctrl>** and drag the file to the **Copies** folder on the **Navigation Pane**. Release the mouse button to copy the file, and then release the **<Ctrl>** key.

14.   On the **Navigation Pane**, click **Copies** underneath the **Computer Essentials** folder. The contents of the **Copies** folder, including the duplicated **Health and Safety** file, now appear in the main **View Pane**.

15.   Select the folder **Computer Essentials** on the **Navigation Pane** and leave the window open for the next lesson.

Driving Lesson 32 - Moving Files

▣ Park and Read

It is good practice at home, in education and at work to keep your electronic files well organised. This usually involves moving related files into appropriately named folders so that you can quickly find information when you need it.

⤺ Manoeuvres

1. Click <u>once</u> on the document file **Financial Report** (<u>not</u> the copy that you created earlier).

2. From the **Toolbar**, click the **Organize** button and select **Cut**. The file is cut and placed in memory (notice that the cut file now appears faded).

3. Open the folder **Reports** and select **Paste** from the **Organize** button. The file is moved from the original folder to this one.

4. Return to the **Computer Essentials** folder to confirm that **Financial Report** is no longer present.

5. Use the same technique to move the **Accounts** file to the **Reports** folder.

ⓘ *If you move a file to a location where a file with the same name already exists, you will be given the option to replace the existing file in the destination folder or rename the copied file (as you will see in the next lesson).*

6. Next, drag and drop the **Bookings** database file onto the **Databases** folder to move it. Notice that the **Move to** cursor appears.

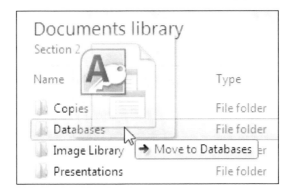

7. Hold down the **<Ctrl>** key on your keyboard as you select the image files **Computer** and **Park View** *together*. Release **<Ctrl>** and drag either file to the **Image Library** folder.

Driving Lesson 32 - Continued

8. Both selected files are moved. Next, <u>expand</u> the **Presentations** folder on the **Navigation Pane** to show the 2 subfolders **Marketing** and **Training**.

9. Drag the files **Holidays**, **Retreat** and **Theme Park** from the **View Pane** to the **Marketing** folder on the **Navigation Pane**.

10. Next, drag the file **Health and Safety** to the **Training** folder. Check that all files have been moved correctly.

11. Move the files **Company News**, **HS Guidelines**, and **Renaissance** to the **Publications** folder. Then, move the **Personnel** file to the **Databases** folder.

12. Create a new folder called **Media Files** in the **Computer Essentials** folder and move the following files into it: **Ocean** and **Tune**.

Documents library
Computer Essentials

Name	Date modified	Type
Copies	20/02/2013 14:33	File folder
Databases	20/02/2013 14:36	File folder
Image Library	20/02/2013 14:35	File folder
Media Files	20/02/2013 14:37	File folder
Presentations	20/02/2013 14:29	File folder
Publications	20/02/2013 14:36	File folder
Reports	20/02/2013 14:34	File folder
Activities.docx	20/02/2013 11:05	Microsoft Word Document
Financial Report - Copy.docx	12/02/2013 09:02	Microsoft Word Document
Meeting.zip	19/02/2013 16:32	Compressed (zipped) Folder
Text.txt	09/08/2012 13:52	Text Document

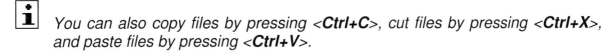

*You can also copy files by pressing <**Ctrl+C**>, cut files by pressing <**Ctrl+X**>, and paste files by pressing <**Ctrl+V**>.*

13. Great, all files are now well organised and will be much easier to find later. You will deal with any remaining files later in this section.

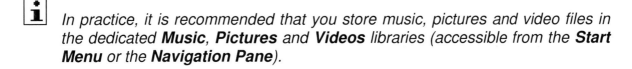

*In practice, it is recommended that you store music, pictures and video files in the dedicated **Music**, **Pictures** and **Videos** libraries (accessible from the **Start Menu** or the **Navigation Pane**).*

Driving Lesson 33 - Organising Folders

▣ Park and Read

You can organise folders using the same techniques used to organise files. However, when you copy or move a folder, it is important to understand that <u>all</u> of its contents – including subfolders – are copied or moved as well.

↱ Manoeuvres

1. With the **Computer Essentials** data files window open from the previous lesson, click <u>once</u> on the folder **Databases** to select it.

2. From the **Toolbar**, click the **Organize** button and select **Copy**. The entire folder is copied and placed in memory.

3. Open the **Copies** folder and select **Paste** from the **Organize** button. The copied folder appears containing a *duplicate* of the original folder's contents.

4. Open the new **Databases** folder to check the *copied* contents. The databases **Bookings** and **Personnel** appear. Return to the **Copies** folder.

5. Try to drag and drop the database file **Bookings** into the folder **Databases** (within the **Copies** folder). As that folder already contains a file with that name, the following dialog box appears.

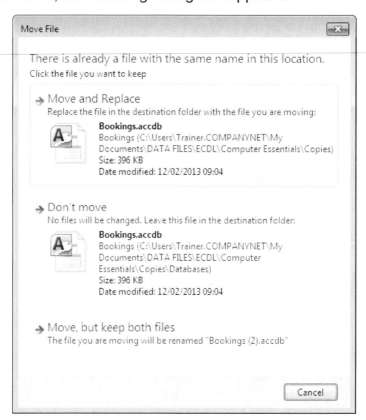

Driving Lesson 33 - Continued

6. Examine the three options available and read their descriptions: **Move and Replace**; **Don't move**; **Move, but keep both files**.

7. Select **Move and Replace** to overwrite the existing file with the copied file.

8. Create a new folder (in the current **Copies** folder) and name it **Backup**. Drag and drop the folder **Databases** into it, along with the files **Computer** and **Health and Safety**.

9. The files and the **Databases** folder (including all of its contents) are moved. Explore the **Backup** folder to confirm this.

i *You can also copy folders by pressing <**Ctrl+C**>, cut folders by pressing <**Ctrl+X**>, and paste folders by pressing <**Ctrl+V**>.*

10. Return to the **Computer Essentials** folder and leave it open for the next lesson.

i *Rather than store hundreds of mixed files in a single folder, use a logical structured hierarchy of folders to help organise your files and make them easier to manage.*

Driving Lesson 34 - Renaming Items

▣ Park and Read

From time to time you may need to change file and folder names as their contents change. It is *always* good practice to give your files and folders sensible and meaningful names. If a file or folder is well labelled, you should not need to open it to find out what it contains.

ℹ️ *Using descriptive file and folder names becomes increasingly important over time. When there are hundreds of files and folders stored on your computer, a well-considered filing structure will allow you to search more efficiently.*

ℹ️ *Care should be taken when renaming files to maintain the correct file extension. If it is changed,* Windows *will not know which application to open the file with.*

Manoeuvres

1. With the **Computer Essentials** data files window open from the previous lesson, click *once* on the document file **Financial Report - Copy**.

2. From the **Organize** menu, click **Rename**. Notice that the file's name (*without* extension) appears highlighted in a text box, ready for editing.

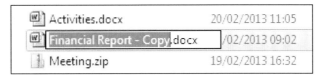

3. Enter **Budget Report** as the new file name and press <**Enter**>. The file's name is changed. Move the file to the **Reports** folder.

4. Right click on the **Media Files** folder to display a drop-down menu.

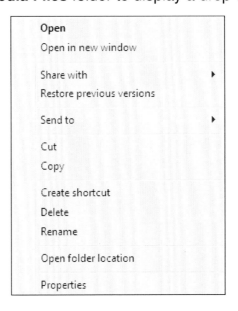

Driving Lesson 34 - Continued

 Right-clicking an object in Windows *usually displays a* **context-sensitive menu** *that can be used to perform the most common actions for that item. The menu is called context-sensitive as the items on it change depending on the object clicked.*

5. Examine the options shown (more may appear on your menu). There are a number of powerful file management shortcuts available here.

 Open in a new window *lets you open the selected folder in a new window. This is sometimes useful when moving files from folder to folder.*

 As you will find out later in this guide, **Create shortcut** *lets you create a link to this folder that can be placed elsewhere (e.g. your* **Desktop***).*

6. For now, click **Rename** and then change the folder name to **Sound and Video**.

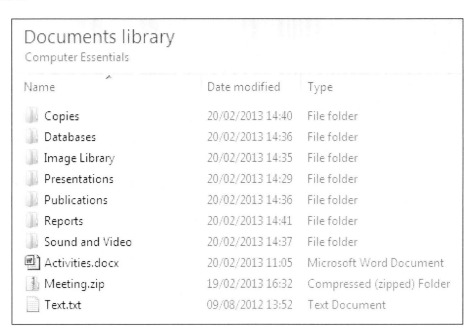

 A very slow double click on a file or folder's name also lets you rename it.

7. Leave the **Computer Essentials** data files window open for the next lesson.

Driving Lesson 35 - Deleting Items

▣ Park and Read

Files and folders can be **deleted** when they are no longer needed. This removes them from your computer and frees up space for other files and programs to use.

↱ Manoeuvres

1. With the **Computer Essentials** data files window open from the previous lesson, click once on the document file **Text**.

2. Press the <**Delete**> key on your keyboard. A prompt appears asking you to confirm that you want to delete this file.

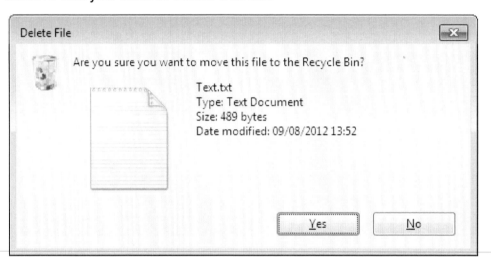

Delete File

Are you sure you want to move this file to the Recycle Bin?

Text.txt
Type: Text Document
Size: 489 bytes
Date modified: 09/08/2012 13:52

         Yes   No

3. Click **Yes**. The file is moved to the **Recycle Bin** (you will find out more about this in the next lesson).

4. Display the **Organize** menu and click **Undo**. Your last action is undone and the **Text** file reappears in the folder.

5. Right click once on the **Text** file and then select **Delete** from the shortcut menu. At the prompt, select **Yes** to move the file to the **Recycle Bin** again.

6. Next, select the **Copies** folder by clicking it once. Then, click the **Organize** button and select **Delete**. At the prompt, select **Yes** to move this folder to the **Recycle Bin**.

ℹ️ *Be careful: if you delete a folder, all of its contents will be deleted too.*

7. Use the **Organize** button to **Undo** the deletion.

8. Select the **Copies** folder once more. Then press <**Delete**> and select **Yes** to move the folder to the **Recycle Bin** again.

Driving Lesson 36 - The Recycle Bin

◫ Park and Read

When files or folders are deleted they are not instantly removed from your computer. Instead, they are placed in a special folder on the **Desktop** called the **Recycle Bin**. Until the **Recycle Bin** is emptied the contents can always be restored to their original locations.

ⓘ *Items deleted from network locations or peripheral storage drives are **not** moved to the **Recycle Bin** – they are deleted <u>immediately</u>!*

⟳ Manoeuvres

1. Minimise the **Computer Essentials** data files window to return to the **Desktop** (or click the **Show Desktop** button on the **Taskbar**). Locate the **Recycle Bin** icon.

Recycle Bin

ⓘ *Notice during this lesson that the icon for the **Recycle Bin** changes depending on whether or not it contains deleted items.*

2. Double-click the **Recycle Bin** icon. The contents of the **Recycle Bin** are displayed in a new window.

ⓘ *The current contents of your **Recycle Bin** will depend on the files and folders you have deleted.*

3. Locate and select the file **Text** that you deleted in the previous lesson. From the **Toolbar**, click the **Restore this item** button.

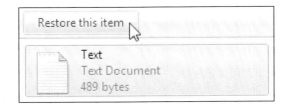

4. The file is removed from the **Recycle Bin** and restored to (i.e. put back in) its original location. Display the **Computer Essentials** data files window again to find the **Text** file.

ⓘ *If the folder that contained the file has also been deleted, the **Recycle Bin** re-creates it.*

Driving Lesson 36 - Continued

5. Delete the **Text** file again and it is moved back into the **Recycle Bin**.

6. On the **Recycle Bin** window, locate and restore the **Copies** folder deleted earlier. The folder and all of its original contents are placed back in the **Computer Essentials** folder.

7. Display the **Computer Essentials** data files window to find the **Copies** folder. Delete it again and it is moved back into the **Recycle Bin**.

8. Return to the **Recycle Bin** window and click **Empty the Recycle Bin** on the **Toolbar**. A prompt appears asking you to confirm the permanent deletion of all items in the folder.

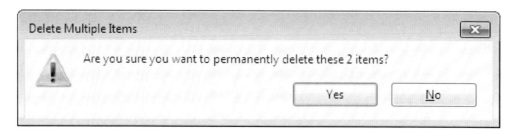

 *You can safely delete any data files or folders that were moved to the **Recycle Bin** in this section.*

9. If you are *absolutely* sure that you do not need any of the other files currently contained in the **Recycle Bin** folder, select **Yes**. Otherwise select **No**.

10. Close the **Recycle Bin** window and minimise the **Computer Essentials** data files window. If you deleted the contents of the **Recycle Bin** the **Desktop** icon will now appear empty.

Recycle Bin

 *You can also empty the contents of the **Recycle Bin** by right-clicking its icon on the **Desktop** and selecting **Empty Recycle Bin**.*

11. Maximise the **Computer Essentials** data files window and leave it open for the next lesson.

Driving Lesson 37 - Item Properties

▣ Park and Read

Every file and folder in *Windows* has a number of simple **properties** which describe those items. Properties include file type, location, size, and dates when the item was created and/or modified.

↱ Manoeuvres

1. Open the **Publications** folder within the **Computer Essentials** data files window.

2. Select the **Company News** file and, using the **Organize** button, select **Properties**. Examine the **Properties** dialog box that appears.

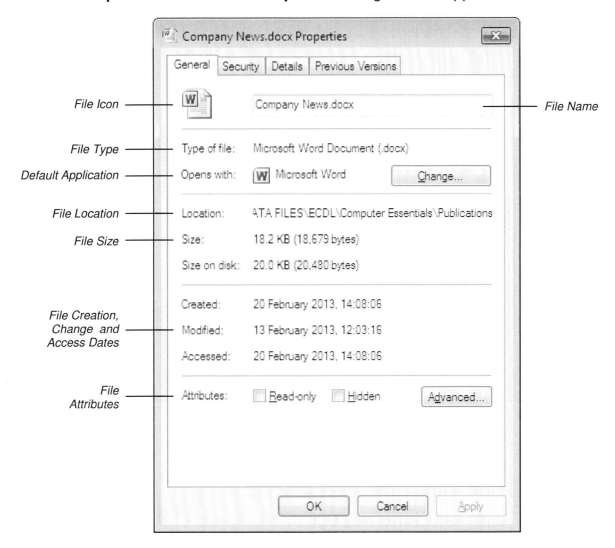

ℹ **Opens with** *indicates the default application that will "open with" this file when it is double-clicked. The* **Change** *button can be used to select another program.*

Driving Lesson 37 - Continued

3.   Notice the **File Name** field. In addition to the techniques described in *Driving Lesson 34*, this can be used to edit the name of the file.

4.   Locate the **Size** property. This describes the total size of the currently selected file.

> **i**   *Refer to the file size table in* Driving Lesson 7 *for more information on how file sizes are measured.*

5.   The useful **Created**, **Modified** and **Accessed** properties indicate when the current file was created, when it was last changed (and saved), and when it was last opened.

6.   Finally, an important and frequently used property of a file's **Attributes** is the **Read-only** checkbox. If this is checked, the selected file can be opened and read but changes cannot be saved. This helps to prevent accidental changes to important files.

> **i**   *Changes to a read-only file can be saved using a different file name. Alternatively, remove the read-only property by deselecting the* **Read-only** *attribute.*

7.   Next, display the **Details** tab and examine the various properties associated with the selected file (you can scroll down to see a full list).

> **i**   *The* **Previous Versions** *tab allows you to access and restore older versions of the current file. This is useful if important information is accidentally deleted.*

8.   Click **Cancel** to close the **Properties** dialog box. Then, return to the **Computer Essentials** folder.

9.   Next, select the folder **Publications** and, using the **Organize** button, select **Properties**. Examine the **Properties** dialog box that appears.

> **i**   *Notice the* **Contains** *value which indicates the number of files and subfolders within the selected folder. The* **Size** *property also refers to the total size of the folder and <u>all</u> of its contents.*

10.   Click the **Cancel** button to close the dialog box.

> **i**   *Right-clicking a file or folder and selecting* **Properties** *will also display the* **Properties** *dialog box.*

11.   Explore the subfolders within the **Computer Essentials** folder and examine the **Properties** of other files and folders.

12.   When you are finished, return to the **Computer Essentials** folder.

Driving Lesson 38 - Searching

▣ Park and Read

Over time you will create and save a lot of files. However, trying to find a specific piece of information amongst all of these files and folders can sometimes be like trying to find a needle in a haystack. Luckily, the *Windows* search features are on hand to help.

ⓘ *The* Windows *search feature is not a replacement for a good, well-designed and meaningfully labelled folder structure.*

Searching for files and folders is achieved using the **Search** box in **Windows Explorer**. Searches act on the contents of the current folder and subfolders only.

↱ Manoeuvres

1. With the **Computer Essentials** data files window open, click once in the **Search** box at the top right and enter the keyword **financial**.

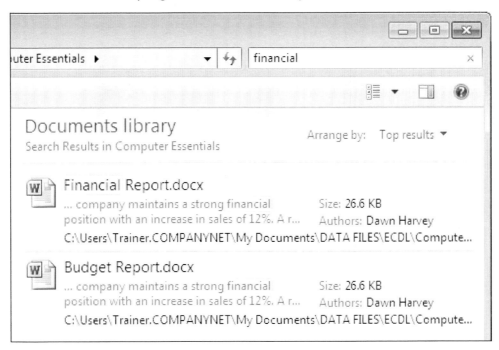

2. As you type, *Windows* starts searching for files and folders matching the keyword and displays the results. The keyword text can appear anywhere in file or folder names or, where applicable, in the actual contents of the files themselves.

ⓘ *As* Windows *performs a search as you type, you sometimes only need to enter the first few letters to produce useful results. However, the more letters you enter, the more specific the results.*

Driving Lesson 38 - Continued

i *Notice that two files are found. The first,* **Financial Report***, contains the keyword* **financial** *in the file name. The second,* **Budget Report***, contains the keyword in the text inside of the file.*

3. To clear the search results click the **Clear** button, ⊠, in the **Search** box (not the window's **Close** button). The full contents of the **Computer Essentials** data files folder reappears.

4. Next, try searching for the keyword **report**. 6 items will be shown. Examine each of the results and see where the keyword was found.

5. Clear the search and then try searching for the keyword **company**. Briefly examine the 26 items discovered.

i *More than one keyword can be used to help narrow a search and produce more specific results.*

6. Clear the search and try searching for the following two keywords: **company news**. 1 file is found.

7. Finally, clear the search and try searching for the following keywords: **health safety**. 2 files are found.

8. Clear the search to restore the full contents of the **Computer Essentials** data files folder.

i *You can also use the search techniques described in this lesson when exploring the contents of data storage media such as CDs and DVDs, USB memory sticks, external hard drives, and even local internal networks.*

i *To perform a more general search of all storage devices connected to your computer, the small text box located at the bottom of the* Windows **Start Menu** *can be used. This can also be used to search for and start programs.*

Driving Lesson 39 - Search Filters

▣ Park and Read

Search Filters can be used to produce more specific results when performing a search. It is possible to search for files of a certain size or type, or those which have been modified on or within specific dates.

☞ Manoeuvres

1. With the **Computer Essentials** data files window open, click once in the **Search** box. Notice the **Add a search filter** buttons that appear.

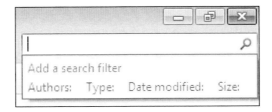

2. Click once on **Type:** and examine the list of file types that appears. Select **.docx** from the list and five files with **.docx** extensions are found and shown (i.e. all *Word* or *WordPad* documents).

ℹ️ *The file types that appear in the **Type:** pop-up menu are based on the contents of the current folder and any subfolders within.*

3. Clear the search and then try searching for files with a **.accdb** extension (i.e. *Access* databases). 2 files are found.

ℹ️ *At the bottom of the **Type:** list are alternative, plain English file types.*

4. Clear the search and then try searching for files with a **.xlsx** extension (i.e. *Excel* spreadsheets). A single file is found.

5. Next, Clear the search and click the **Date modified** button. The pop-up that appears can be used to search for files and folders that have been changed on a specific date or range of dates.

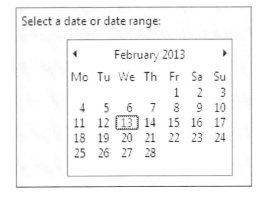

Driving Lesson 39 - Continued

6.   You can select specific days on the calendar to view items modified on that date. Try clicking on today's date to see items modified today (if any).

i   *A range of dates can also be selected by clicking and dragging across multiple consecutive days on the calendar.*

7.   Experiment by selecting some of the range shortcuts that appear below the calendar (e.g. **A long time ago**, **Last week**, **Yesterday**).

i   *The search results depend on the date you installed the data files for this guide.*

8.   Clear the search and click the **Size** button.

9.   From the pop-up menu that appears, select **Small (10 - 100 KB)**. 10 files are found. Notice that their **Size** properties are between **10 KB** and **100 KB**.

i   *Search keywords and filters can be combined to produce better search results.*

10.   Clear the search and enter the keyword **health**. 3 files are found. Click the **Size:** filter button and select **Medium (100 Kb - 1 Mb)**. Two files are found that match *both* criteria.

11.   Clear the search and enter the keyword **park**. 3 files are found. Click the **Type:** filter button and select **.jpg**. Now only a single image file is found.

12.   Next, try searching for **Small** *Word* documents (**.docx**) matching the keyword **report**. You should find 3 files.

i   *When searching, the useful asterisk, *, **wildcard** symbol can also be used in place of one or more characters in a keyword. For example, the search **yo*** will find matches with the words York, yolk, yoga, and so on.*

13.   Search for the following: **com*ews**. The file **Company News** should be found.

14.   Try another search using the following criteria: ***counts**. The file **Accounts** should be found.

15.   Finally, try searching for the following: ***.docx**. All five *Word* documents are found again.

16.   Feel free to experiment with the asterisk wildcard symbol. It can be a useful tool for narrowing search results.

17.   When you are finished, close the **Computer Essentials** window and return to the **Desktop**.

Driving Lesson 40 - Revision

▣ Park and Read

At the end of every section you get the chance to complete one or more revision exercises to develop your skills and prepare you for your ECDL certification test. You should aim to complete the following steps without referring back to the previous lessons.

⟰ Manoeuvres

1. Open the **Documents** folder and navigate to the **Computer Essentials** data files folder.

2. Create a copy of the **Reports** folder and all of its contents.

3. Rename the copy **Reports Backup**.

4. Create a new folder called **Revision** and move the **Reports Backup** folder (and all of its contents) into it.

5. Use the **Navigation Pane** to open the **Image Library** folder. Select and copy the two files within at the same time.

6. Return to the new **Revision** folder and paste duplicates of the two copied files.

7. Rename the **Computer** file **Desktop PC**.

8. Change the view to **Large Icons**. Notice that small thumbnail previews of the file's contents now appear.

9. Restore the view to **Details** view.

10. Delete the file **Park View** and the folder **Reports Backup**.

11. The file **Park View** and the folder **Reports Backup** were deleted in error. Restore both from the **Recycle Bin** to their original location.

12. View the **Properties** for the **Reports Backup** folder. How many files does this folder contain?

13. Open the **Reports Backup** folder and view the **Properties** for the **Financial Report** document.

14. What is the **Financial Report** document's **Size**?

15. Delete the **Revision** folder and all of its contents.

16. Somewhere within the **Computer Essentials** folder is a file called **Retreat**. Find it using the **Search** box.

17. What kind of file is **Retreat**?

Driving Lesson 40 - Continued

18. Search for all files in the **Computer Essentials** folder that are between **100KB** and **1MB** (**Medium** size). How many results are there?

19. Close any open windows

20. Provided that there are no deleted files or folders that you *may* need to restore in the future, empty the **Recycle Bin**.

i   *Sample answers can be found at the back of the guide.*

i   *Now complete the **Record of Achievement Matrix** at the back of the guide. You should only move on when confident with the topics and features described in this section.*

Section 4
Working with Text

By the end of this section you should be able to:

Start and close the WordPad program

Recognise common program features

Create text-based documents

Save documents

Open documents

Use cut, copy and paste

Access recently used file lists

Capture screen images

Work through the **Driving Lessons** in this section to gain an understanding of the above features.

For each **Driving Lesson**, read all of the **Park and Read** instructions and then perform the numbered steps of the **Manoeuvres**. Complete the **Revision** exercise(s) at the end of the section to test your knowledge.

Driving Lesson 41 - WordPad

▣ Park and Read

WordPad is a basic word-processing program that can be used to create, edit, format, save and print text-based documents. It is one of the many built-in utilities installed with *Windows*.

ⓘ WordPad *should not be confused with the more advanced* Microsoft Word, *a professional word-processing application available as part of the* Microsoft Office *suite*.

Manoeuvres

1. Click the **Start** button and then select **All Programs** to display a list of all the programs currently installed on your computer.

2. Click the **Accessories** folder once to open it. From the list of programs that appears, locate and click once on **WordPad** to start the program. After a moment, the program's user interface will appear.

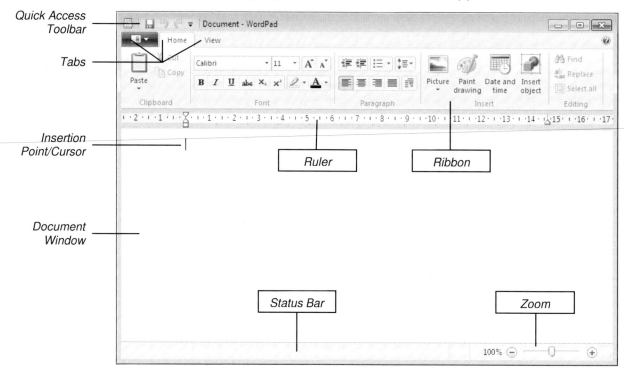

ⓘ *You can also open WordPad by searching for and selecting its name using the Windows search feature (available on the **Start Menu**). If an icon for WordPad is available on the **Desktop**, you can double-click this to launch the program.*

3. Familiarise yourself with the main parts of the *WordPad* window, as described overleaf.

Driving Lesson 41 - Continued

Ribbon	The **Ribbon** is a collection of program commands that appears across the top of the window. Commands are placed into related groups so that they are easier to find.
Tabs	Each tab, when clicked, shows a different set of program commands on the **Ribbon** or on a separate drop-down menu.
Quick Access Toolbar	Frequently used commands are placed here such as **Save**, **Undo** and **Redo**.
Document Window	The main editing window is where you create, edit and read word-processed documents.
Status Bar	Useful program information and notifications appear here.
Zoom	The **Zoom** slider can be used to zoom the **Document Window** in/out and see more/less detail in a document.

i *Most Microsoft Office programs use the same basic screen layout.*

4. Examine the **Ribbon**. The **Home** tab is currently selected and a number of program commands are shown.

i *This guide introduces basic document creation, opening, printing and saving techniques. It does not cover more advanced word-processing skills such as text editing, font formatting and paragraph alignment.*

5. Click the **View** tab on the **Ribbon**. Another set of program commands for changing view settings appears, again arranged into related groups.

6. Click the special **WordPad** tab, ▣▾, to reveal a number of program features for creating, saving, opening and printing documents. You will learn more about these in later lessons. For now, click the **WordPad** tab again to close the menu.

i *Notice the **WordPad Help** button located towards the top-right corner of the WordPad screen. This can be used to open the **Windows Help and Support** window to find out more about the features and capabilities of WordPad.*

7. To close *WordPad*, click once on the program's **Close** button, ✕.

8. If you are prompted to save any changes, select **Don't Save**. The program is closed.

Driving Lesson 42 - Entering Text

▣ Park and Read

In a word processing program, any key pressed on an ICT device's keyboard appears in the document at the **insertion point** (where the **cursor** flashes). Each letter, number or symbol typed in is called a **character**.

Entering text into a document is easy| ——— *Flashing Cursor*

The cursor can be moved to any place where text *already* exists by pointing and clicking (or by using the arrow keys on the keyboard). New text that you type is inserted at the cursor position, and text that is already there can be deleted using the <**Delete**> or <**Backspace**> keys.

ℹ️ *The <**Delete**> key removes characters one at a time to the right of the cursor. The <**Backspace**> key removes characters one at a time to the left. The layout of your keyboard may appear differently to that shown above.*

When a line of text reaches the right edge of the area in which you can type, it will automatically move onto the next line (this is called **word wrap**). You only need to press <**Enter**> if you want to move onto a new line before you reach the end of the current one. This is called a **paragraph break** as it is used to break the current line of text and start a new paragraph.

ℹ️ *A paragraph is a block of text that is made up from one or more related sentences that are grouped together. New paragraphs always start on a new line.*

⟳ Manoeuvres

1.   Using the **Start Menu**, locate and start the *WordPad* program.

ℹ️ *The* WordPad *window can be moved, resized, scrolled, minimised, maximised and closed like any other window.*

Driving Lesson 42 - Continued

2.   Notice that the cursor is currently flashing in the top left of the **Document Window**, waiting for you to begin entering text. If it is not, click once anywhere in the **Document Window**.

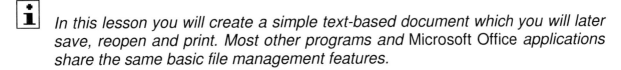 *In this lesson you will create a simple text-based document which you will later save, reopen and print. Most other programs and* Microsoft Office *applications share the same basic file management features.*

3.   Text will always appear at the position of the cursor (i.e. the insertion point). Using your keyboard, type the following:

Welcome to Big Planet Zoo!

Set in 95 acres of parkland, the zoo is located 4 miles north of Learnersville. There are lots of things to do during a visit. As well as meeting over 300 rare and beautiful animals, you can also enjoy many events and activities.

We strive to help ensure the survival of many threatened animal species and work in partnership with other zoos and conservation projects worldwide.

 ***Margins*** *determine the distance between the text and the edges of a page. These are shown as shaded areas on the* ***Ruler****. As the text you enter reaches the margins it automatically wraps to the line below.*

Margin ────── Welcome to Big Planet Zoo!

*Only use the <**Enter**> key to start a new paragraph. To type a capital letter, hold down the <**Shift**> key.*

If you make a mistake, the **Undo** *button, ⤺ , on the* ***Quick Access Toolbar*** *allows you to undo changes and correct mistakes by stepping back through each action performed (one step at a time).*

4.   Leave the new document open for the next lesson.

Driving Lesson 43 - Saving Documents

▣ Park and Read

Documents created in *WordPad* can be saved to a storage device so that they can be opened and used again later.

⌒ Manoeuvres

1. To save the current document, click the *WordPad* tab, 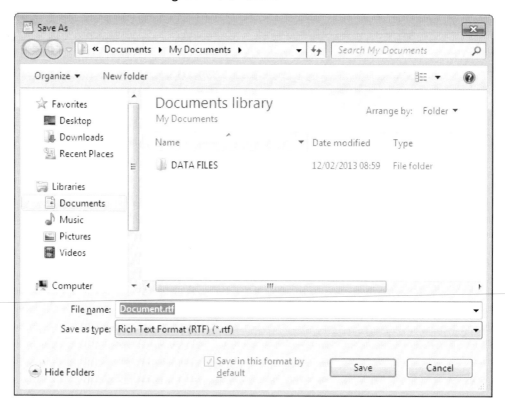 and select **Save**. The **Save As** dialog box is shown.

ℹ️ *Alternatively, click the **Save** button,* 🖫 *on the **Quick Access Toolbar** or use the key press <**Ctrl S**> to display the **Save As** dialog box.*

2. Your **Documents** library is shown by default. Navigate to the **Computer Essentials** folder (i.e. **DATA FILES/ECDL/Computer Essentials**).

3. Click once in the **File name** box and notice that the default text, **Document.rtf**, is selected. Enter the new name **zoo** to overtype this.

ℹ️ *You do not need to add a file extension. If missing, this will be automatically added when the file is saved, depending on the file type selected in the **Save as type** drop-down box. The default file type chosen is usually best, but other formats can be selected if the file needs to be used later in a different program.*

Driving Lesson 43 - Continued

4. Make sure **Rich Text Format (RTF)** is selected in the **Save as type** drop-down menu. This will save the document as an RTF file.

i *Recall from Driving Lesson 27 that an RTF file is a document that supports "rich" text formatting.*

5. Click the **Save** button to save this file to the **Computer Essentials** folder. The **Save As** dialog box is automatically closed.

i *The **Title Bar** across the top of the window now displays the current document's file name and the program name, **zoo.rtf - WordPad**.*

6. Create a new paragraph at the end of the document and type the following text:

   The zoo is open every day of the year and is accessible to visitors with special needs. Parking for 1500 cars is also available at the east side of the park.

7. To save these changes, click the *WordPad* tab, , and select **Save** (or click the **Save** button on the **Quick Access Toolbar** again). The file is saved again with the *same* file name, overwriting the contents of the previously saved file.

i *Saving the document again will overwrite the contents of the last saved file. You will not be prompted to enter another file name. If you wish to save the file with a different name, use **Save as** instead.*

8. Close *WordPad*. The open file **zoo** is closed also.

i *If there are any unsaved changes made to a document when WordPad is closed, you will be prompted to save those changes. This is a common feature of most programs.*

9. Use the **Start Menu** to open the **Documents** window. Then, navigate to the **Computer Essentials** folder to find the **zoo** file in the **View Pane**.

Activities.docx	20/02/2013 11:05	Microsoft Word Document
Meeting.zip	19/02/2013 16:32	Compressed (zipped) Folder
zoo.rtf	20/02/2013 14:53	Rich Text Format

10. Notice the document icon, , and the file type of the new **zoo** file: **Rich Text Format**.

11. Close the **Documents** window and return to the **Desktop**.

Driving Lesson 44 - Opening Documents

🄿 Park and Read

Most text files and documents saved on a storage device can be opened, read and edited from within *WordPad*.

🄬 Manoeuvres

1. Using the **Start Menu**, start the *WordPad* program.

2. Next, click the *WordPad* tab, [▣▼] and select **Open**. The **Open** dialog box is shown.

> 🄸 *Alternatively, press <**Ctrl O**> to display the **Open** dialog box.*

3. Your **Documents** library is again shown by default. Navigate to the **Computer Essentials** folder to find the **zoo** document saved earlier.

> 🄸 *It is important to realise that only folders and file types compatible with WordPad are shown by default. To show other file types, the button currently labelled **All Wordpad Documents** can be used.*

4. Click once to select the file **zoo**. Then, click the **Open** button to open the file and display the contents in the **Document Window**, ready for editing.

> 🄸 *Alternatively, you can double-click the file to open it from the **Open** dialog box.*

5. Use the **Open** command again to display the **Open** dialog box.

6. This time, open the document **Activities**. This document contains a list of events for an upcoming activity weekend. Notice the font-formatting that has been applied.

> 🄸 *Opening a document in WordPad automatically closes the previously open file (prompting to save changes first, if necessary). Other programs may be able to open more than one file at once.*

> 🄸 *Recall that scrollbars allow you to move around a page of information that is too large to fit on your screen at once. If the **Activities** document is too long to appear fully in the **Document Window**, use the scrollbar to view all of the text.*

7. Leave *WordPad* and the **Activities** file open for the next lesson.

> 🄸 *Documents and other file types can also be opened by double-clicking them in **Windows Explorer**. You will see how to do this later in the guide.*

Driving Lesson 45 - Cut, Copy and Paste

Park and Read

The **cut**, **copy** and **paste** commands allow text to be moved around a document from one place to another quickly and easily. When you cut text, it is removed from its original location; when you copy it, the original is left untouched.

Words, lines and one or more paragraphs of text can also be copied and pasted between documents (and even into other programs).

Manoeuvres

1. The **Activities** document should still be open from the previous lesson. You are now going to make a number of changes to it.

2. Double-click the word **Introduction** (below **Day 1**) to select it.

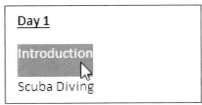

Double-clicking is a useful technique for quickly selecting a single word of text. Alternatively, you can simply click and drag over the word to select it.

3. Click the **Copy** button in the **Clipboard** group on the **Ribbon**, 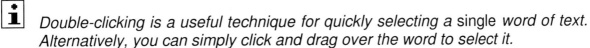. The text is copied.

*Text that is cut or copied is temporarily placed in a special area of memory called the **Clipboard**. This only supports one cut or copy operation at a time; a second will replace the first.*

4. Click once on the blank line below **Day 2** to place the cursor.

5. Then, click the **Paste** button on the **Ribbon** to insert the copied text into the document at the cursor's position (click the **Paste** button's icon, not the drop-down arrow).

6. Note that the original text is left unchanged.

Driving Lesson 45 - Continued

i *You can paste cut and copied text as many times as you like.*

7. Copy **Rafting** from **Day 1** and paste it at the end of the document (i.e. after **Assault Course** in **Day 2**).

8. Next, triple-click (by quickly clicking the left mouse button three times) the text **Safety Briefing** to select both words.

i *Triple-clicking is a useful technique for quickly selecting a whole line or paragraph of text. Alternatively, click and drag over the words to select them.*

9. This time, click the **Cut** button on the **Ribbon**, ✂ Cut . The text is cut from the document and placed onto the **Clipboard**.

10. Position the cursor *before* the text **Scuba Diving** (do not select it). Click **Paste**. The cut text is inserted back into the document at the location of the cursor.

11. Cut the item **Certificate Presentation**. Then, create a new line (using <**Enter**>) *after* **Rafting** and paste the cut text.

12. Using cut and paste, swap the activities **Advanced Sailing** in **Day 1** with **Beginner's Sailing** in **Day 2**.

Day 1
Introduction
Safety Briefing
Scuba Diving
Rafting
Beginner's Sailing
Mountain Biking
Day 2
Introduction
Advanced Sailing
Assault Course
Rafting
Certificate Presentation

Driving Lesson 45 - Continued

i   *Text can also be cut, copied and pasted <u>between</u> documents.*

13.   Press <**Ctrl A**> to select all of the text in the document. Then, click the **Copy** button.

14.   Using the **Start Menu**, open a second instance of *WordPad*. With the cursor flashing in the **Document Window**, **Paste** the contents of the **Clipboard** into the new document.

i   *Notice that the text's formatting is preserved.*

15.   On a blank line directly below **Certificate Presentation**, enter the text **Prize Giving Ceremony**.

16.   Select and *copy* the new line.

17.   Close the new document <u>without</u> saving changes, returning to the original **Activities** document.

i   *Text placed on the **Clipboard** remains available to paste even when the document it was cut or copied from has been closed.*

18.   Paste the copied text **Prize Giving Ceremony** at the end of the document (i.e. below **Certificate Presentation**).

19.   The document is now complete. Use **Save as** from the **WordPad** tab to save the file as **team building** in the **Computer Essentials** folder.

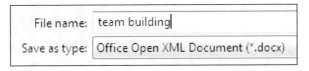

20.   Leave the document open for the next lesson.

i   *Although this lesson has focussed on cutting, copying and pasting text, the same techniques apply to other items such as numbers, pictures, charts and other editable objects.*

Driving Lesson 46 - Printing Documents

▣ Park and Read

It is an easy task to print documents from *WordPad*. Page setup options can be chosen and a preview of the printed page shown before printing.

↱ Manoeuvres

1. With the document **team building** open, click the **WordPad** tab. From the options that appear, place the mouse pointer over **Print** <u>without</u> clicking. Examine the options that appear.

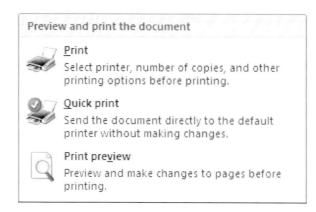

2. Click **Print preview** to see a small preview of the document as it will look when printed.

3. Move the mouse pointer over the page and it changes to the magnifier cursor, ⚲. Click once on the document to zoom in and take a closer look.

4. Click again to zoom back out.

i *If the document runs to more than one page then the **Next page** and **Previous page** buttons on the **Ribbon** can be used. **Two pages** in the **Zoom** group can also be used to show two pages of the document at once.*

5. Click the **Page setup** button to display the **Page Setup** dialog box. This can be used to set margins, paper size and page orientation.

i *The **Left**, **Right**, **Top** and **Bottom** margins can be used to add or decrease space around the document's text. The **Orientation** settings allow you to select which direction to create and print a document: **Portrait** (upright) or **Landscape** (sideways).*

i *Normally, **A4** documents are created in **Portrait** mode. This is the default setting and the orientation that you will use most often. **Landscape** is useful for creative documents such as brochures and newsletters.*

Driving Lesson 46 - Continued

6. To demonstrate the effect of altering page setup, enter **30** in the boxes for **Left**, **Right**, **Top** and **Bottom** margins. This gives the document a consistent space of 30 millimetres between the text and all four edges of the page.

7. To rotate the page, select **Landscape** from **Orientation**.

Orientation	Margins (millimeters)		
○ Portrait	Left: 30	Right:	30
◉ Landscape	Top: 30	Bottom:	30

8. Click **OK** and observe the effect. The document now runs to 2 pages. Use the **Next page** and **Previous page** buttons to view both.

9. Click the **Page setup** button to display the **Page Setup** dialog box again. Restore the page **Orientation** to **Portrait** and click **OK**.

10. Click the **Print** button to display the **Print** dialog box. Examine the settings and options shown.

[i] *The* ***Print*** *dialog box can also be displayed by selecting* ***Print*** *from the* ***WordPad*** *tab or by using the key press* ***<Ctrl P>***.

11. The printers that appear in the **Select Printer** box depend on the printers available to you. Choose the printer you would like to print to from the **Printer** drop-down button.

[i] *In work and education you may have access to many printers. Try to find the name of the one closest to you. In some situations you may also be charged for printing, so be careful what you print.*

[i] *You will find out more about printers and their settings in Section 8.*

[i] *The* ***Preferences*** *button, if available, can also be used to access settings specific to the selected printer (e.g. colour settings, print quality, two-sided printing, etc.).*

12. Make sure **Page Range** is set to **All** and **Number of copies** is **1**. This will print a single copy of all pages in the document.

13. Click the **Print** button. A copy of the document is sent to your chosen printer and *WordPad* automatically returns to the main document view.

14. Save the document and leave *WordPad* open for the next lesson.

[i] *Most* Windows *programs print using the same techniques described here.*

Driving Lesson 47 - Taking Screenshots

▣ Park and Read

Pressing the **Print Screen** key on your keyboard will take a snapshot picture of your entire screen's display and all of its contents. You can then paste this into a document in order to save or print it. This technique is really useful for gathering evidence of your work.

⬧ Manoeuvres

1. Using the *WordPad* tab, click **New** to create a new, blank document. The **team building** document will be closed automatically (be sure to save any changes if prompted to do so).

2. Minimise *WordPad* so that only your *Windows* **Desktop** is visible.

3. Locate and press the <**Print Screen**> key on your keyboard. It is usually located towards the top right of the keyboard (and may be labelled slightly differently, e.g. <**Prt Scn**>).

4. Nothing appears to happen, but in fact a snapshot of your screen has been captured and placed in memory. Return to *WordPad*.

5. With the cursor flashing at the top left of your document, click the **Paste** button to insert a screenshot of your **Desktop**.

ℹ *The screenshot can be resized by clicking on it and then dragging the small square "resize handles", ▪, that appear.*

6. Click once to select the image and display the resize handles. Try resizing the image and observe the effect.

7. With the image still selected, press <**Delete**> to remove it.

8. Next, using the **Start Menu**, open the **Computer** window. Make sure the window is *not* maximised.

ℹ *Holding down the <**Alt**> key and pressing <**Print Screen**> will only capture the active window or dialog box.*

9. Press <**Alt**> and <**Print Screen**> together. A snapshot of the active window *only* has been captured and placed in memory.

10. Close the **Computer** window and return to *WordPad*.

11. With the cursor flashing at the top left of your document, click the **Paste** button to insert the screenshot.

12. Save the document as **screen capture** and close *WordPad*.

Driving Lesson 48 - Recently Used Files

🄿 Park and Read

When you save or open a file in a program, that action is usually recorded and displayed in a **Recent** history list. This allows you to access and open recently used files quicker next time.

ⓘ Windows *also maintains its own list of recently used files for each individual application.*

🄬 Manoeuvres

1. Using the **Start Menu**, start the *WordPad* program.

2. Next, click the *WordPad* tab, . Notice the list of **Recent documents** that appears on the right.

	Recent documents
New	
	1 screen capture.docx
Open	2 team building.docx
	3 Activities.docx
Save	4 zoo.rtf

ⓘ *Your list of recent documents may appear differently. Most programs, including those in the* Microsoft Office *suite, maintain a list similar to this.*

3. Click the entry for **team building** to open that document.

4. Experiment by opening other documents from the **Recent document** list. When you are finished, close *WordPad*.

5. Next, display the **Start Menu**. The program shortcuts that appear on the left of the menu change depending on the programs you have used most recently. The small arrows to the right of some, ▸, provide access to most recently used files for those programs.

6. If there is an entry for *WordPad*, click the small arrow to view a useful list of files opened by that program recently.

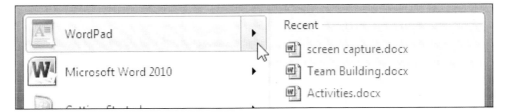

7. If available, try selecting items from this list to open them. When you are finished, close <u>all</u> instances of the *WordPad* program.

Driving Lesson 49 - Revision

▣ Park and Read

At the end of every section you get the chance to complete one or more revision exercises to develop your skills and prepare you for your ECDL certification test. You should aim to complete the following steps without referring back to the previous lessons.

⌐ Manoeuvres

1. Start the *WordPad* program and a new, blank document. Enter the following text:

    The Calculator is a basic Windows program that can be used to perform simple calculations.

2. Save the document as an RTF file named **revision1** in the **Computer Essentials** folder.

3. Next, copy *all* of the text in the document.

4. Start a new document and paste the copied text into it

5. Save the new document as an RTF file named **revision2**.

6. Print a *single* copy of the document in **Portrait** mode (using *WordPad's* default **Page Setup** settings).

7. Close *WordPad*.

8. Using the **Start Menu**, open *Calculator* from the **Accessories** folder and take a screenshot of <u>only this program</u>.

ℹ️ *Hint: use <**Alt**> and <**Print Screen**> together.*

9. Close the *Calculator* program and open the document **revision1** (using either *WordPad's* **Open** command or a "recently used files" list).

10. Then, paste the screenshot at the end of the document.

11. Save the document as **revision3** and close *WordPad*.

12. Delete the files **revision1**, **revision2** and **revision3**.

13. Close any open windows and programs.

ℹ️ *Now complete the **Record of Achievement Matrix** at the back of the guide. You should only move on when confident with the topics and features described in this section.*

Section 5
Icons and Shortcuts

By the end of this section you should be able to:

Open files in their default programs

Create, edit and delete shortcuts

Select and move Desktop icons

Arrange Desktop icons

Work through the **Driving Lessons** in this section to gain an understanding of the above features.

For each **Driving Lesson**, read all of the **Park and Read** instructions and then perform the numbered steps of the **Manoeuvres**. Complete the **Revision** exercise(s) at the end of the section to test your knowledge.

Driving Lesson 50 - Default Programs

▣ Park and Read

A file can be opened from **Windows Explorer** (or the **Desktop**) by double clicking it. The program *best suited* to open and work with that type of file is automatically started.

> **i** *The program that starts depends on the type of file that has been double clicked (as defined by its file extension). For example, double clicking a file with a **.docx** extension will usually start Microsoft Word, double clicking a **.xlsx** file will start Excel, and so on. This is why it is important to maintain the correct file extensions when renaming files.*

> **i** *If a file type does not have a default program associated with it, Windows will ask you to select one from a list of recommended programs.*

⌒ Manoeuvres

1. Open the **Documents** folder and navigate to the **Computer Essentials** data files folder.

2. Double-click the file **Activities**. The program best suited to handling documents of this type is started and the file opened.

> **i** *If Microsoft Office is present on your computer, the application Microsoft Word will probably open the file. If not, the program WordPad may be used.*

3. Close the **Activities** file <u>and</u> the program that opened it.

4. Explore the subfolders in the **Computer Essentials** folder. Double-click different types of files and observe the default programs used to open them.

> **i** *To open a file in a specific program, simply right-click it and select **Open with**. From the submenu that appears, select the program you would like to use. The default program for files of that type can also be changed here.*

5. When you are finished, close any open programs and then close the **Computer Essentials** window.

Driving Lesson 51 - Shortcuts

▣ Park and Read

Small files called **shortcuts** can be created that provide quick and easy access to commonly used (or time-consuming to access) programs, files and folders. They are like "sign posts" and can be easily moved, renamed and deleted without affecting the items they point to.

↱ Manoeuvres

1. To create a shortcut to the *Calculator* program, display the **Start Menu** and select **All Programs**. Expand the **Accessories** folder and locate the *Calculator* entry.

2. Place your mouse pointer over **Calculator** and right click. From the shortcut menu that appears, select **Send To | Desktop (create shortcut)**.

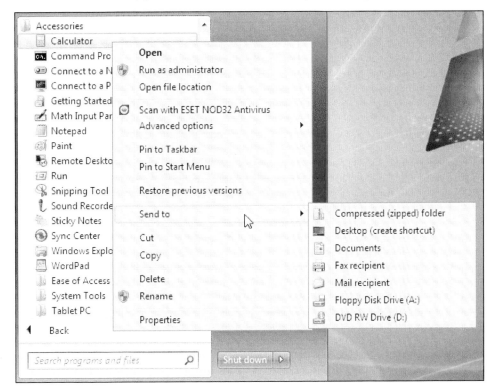

ⓘ *Notice that shortcuts can also be "pinned" to the **Taskbar** or **Start Menu** for easier access.*

3. Click the **Start** button to close the **Start Menu**. Notice that a new shortcut to the *Calculator* program has appeared on the **Desktop**.

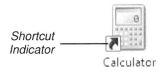

Shortcut Indicator
Calculator

Driving Lesson 51 - Continued

*Although shortcuts can be placed anywhere in your personal folders, they are most often used to create **Desktop** icons. A small arrow, , is used to indicate that the icon is a shortcut.*

4. Double-click the **Calculator** shortcut. The program it points to is run and the *Calculator* program starts.

5. Close the *Calculator* program.

6. Next, create a shortcut on the **Desktop** to the *WordPad* program. Test the shortcut and then close the *WordPad* program that starts.

7. Open your **Documents** library and navigate to the **Computer Essentials** folder. Right click the **Presentations** folder and, again, select **Send to | Desktop (create shortcut)**. A new shortcut is created on the **Desktop** to the **Presentations** folder.

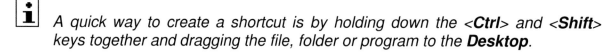

*A quick way to create a shortcut is by holding down the <**Ctrl**> and <**Shift**> keys together and dragging the file, folder or program to the **Desktop**.*

8. Similarly, create a shortcut on the **Desktop** to the **Activities** file.

9. Close the **Computer Essentials** window and return to the **Desktop**. Notice the shortcut icons that are now present.

Calculator   WordPad   Presentations   Activities.d...
                             - Shortcut   - Shortcut

10. Test the shortcut to the **Presentations** folder. Close the window that appears.

11. Likewise, test the shortcut to the **Activities** document. Then close the file and the application used to open it.

Shortcuts can be renamed and deleted without affecting the file, folder or program they point to.

12. Right click the shortcut labelled **Presentations - Shortcut** and select **Rename** from the menu that appears.

13. Type **PowerPoint Files** and press <**Enter**> to rename the shortcut.

14. Using the same technique, change **Activities.docx - Shortcut** to **Events**.

15. Finally, click once to select the **WordPad** shortcut. Then press the <**Delete**> key to delete it (the original program will not be affected).

16. Click **Yes** to confirm the deletion and remove the shortcut.

Driving Lesson 52 - Arranging Icons

▣ Park and Read

Icons and shortcuts on the **Desktop** can be moved by simply clicking and dragging. They can also be sorted and automatically arranged into a tidy grid pattern.

↱ Manoeuvres

1. Click and drag the **Calculator** shortcut to any other empty location on the **Desktop**. Release the mouse button to drop it.

ℹ️ *By default, **Desktop** icons "snap" to an invisible grid when dragged and dropped. This helps to keep icons well arranged and prevents overlapping.*

2. Experiment by dragging icons around the **Desktop**. Be careful not to drop one icon onto another as this can have undesired consequences.

ℹ️ *For example, files will be opened by dragging and dropping them onto an application's shortcut icon. Items dropped in the **Recycle Bin** will be deleted.*

3. Right-click an empty part of the **Desktop** to display a pop-up menu. From the options that appear, select **Sort by | Name**.

4. All of the icons on the **Desktop** are sorted into alphabetical order and arranged in a neat grid pattern.

ℹ️ *Desktop icons can be auto-arranged so that they are always kept in order. This feature can be turned on or off by selecting **View | Auto arrange icons**.*

5. Try arranging icons by **Size**, **Item type** and **Date modified**. Finally, sort the icons by **Name** to restore their original order.

6. Right-click an empty part of the **Desktop** to display the pop-up menu again. This time, select **View | Large icons**. Observe the effect.

7. Try viewing **Desktop** contents as **Small icons**, and then restore the view to **Medium icons**.

ℹ️ *Never move program files from their installation folders to another location. This will usually cause the program to stop working. Only shortcuts to program files (and files and folders you create) can be moved, renamed and deleted safely.*

Driving Lesson 53 - Revision

▣ Park and Read

At the end of every section you get the chance to complete one or more revision exercises to develop your skills and prepare you for your ECDL certification test. You should aim to complete the following steps without referring back to the previous lessons.

⌐ Manoeuvres

1. Double-click the **Desktop** shortcut labelled **Events** to open the linked document in its default program.

2. Close the file and the program that opened it.

3. Delete the **Events** shortcut.

4. Double-click the shortcut **Calculator** to open the program it links to.

5. Close the *Calculator* program that opens.

6. Delete the **Calculator** shortcut.

7. Double-click the shortcut labelled **PowerPoint Files**. When the **Presentations** folder appears, open the **Marketing** subfolder.

8. Create a shortcut on the **Desktop** to the **Holidays** file.

9. Close the **Marketing** window.

10. Rename the **Desktop** shortcut labelled **Holidays.pptx - Shortcut** to **Adventures.**

11. Double-click the **Adventures** shortcut to open the presentation that it links to.

12. Close the file and the program that opened it.

13. Next, create new **Desktop** shortcuts to the **Paint** and **Notepad** programs found in the **Accessories** folder.

14. Practise moving icons around the **Desktop** using click and drag.

15. Delete the **PowerPoint Files** and the **Adventures** shortcut. Then, delete the **Paint** and **Notepad** shortcuts.

16. Finally, sort any remaining **Desktop** icons by name.

ⓘ *Now complete the **Record of Achievement Matrix** at the back of the guide. You should only move on when confident with the topics and features described in this section.*

Section 6
Storage Space

By the end of this section you should be able to:

Access and use storage devices

View used and available space

Understand file compression

Compress and edit files

Extract compressed files

Work through the **Driving Lessons** in this section to gain an understanding of the above features.

For each **Driving Lesson**, read all of the **Park and Read** instructions and then perform the numbered steps of the **Manoeuvres**. Complete the **Revision** exercise(s) at the end of the section to test your knowledge.

Driving Lesson 54 - Storage Space

▣ Park and Read

Nearly all ICT computing devices have some form of local or removable storage space for saving files to. However, as this space is usually limited, it is useful to see how much space is available *before* moving large files on to it.

🛈 *You should always aim to manage your storage space effectively by deleting old and unwanted files.*

🛈 *Multimedia files in particular (e.g. images, videos and sound files) can occupy huge amounts of disk space! Even large hard drives can run out of space.*

↱ Manoeuvres

1.   Click the **Start** button and then click **Computer** from the right of the **Start Menu**.

2.   The **Computer** view is opened. This view shows any and all storage devices that are currently connected to your computer.

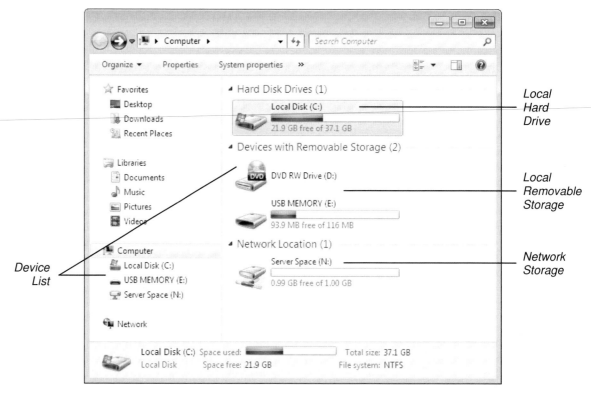

🛈 *Depending on how your computer is set up, you may see a different list of storage devices. "Local" refers to devices connected directly to your computer.*

3.   Examine the drive icons that appear in both the **Navigation Pane** and **View Pane**. Notice that labels describe each device type and location.

Driving Lesson 54 - Continued

4.   Locate and click once on the hard disk drive labelled **Local Disk (C:)**.

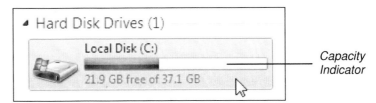

Capacity Indicator

 *Your local hard disk drive may be labelled slightly differently. In the unlikely event that you do not have a **Local Disk (C:)**, simply choose another device.*

5.   Notice that *Windows* provides a brief **Capacity Indicator** that shows available space on a device. This information is repeated on the **Details Pane**.

 ***Local Disk (C:)** is the default storage device for most computers. It is where all of the operating system and program files are stored.*

 *Windows gives all storage devices attached to a computer a unique alphabetical identifier known as a **drive letter** (which follows the drive's name in brackets). Drive letters **A** and **B** are reserved for older floppy disk drives, **C** is usually reserved for the computer's default storage device, and **D** upwards is assigned to other storage and removable disk drives as they are added.*

6.   Right-click the drive **Local Disk (C:)** and select **Properties**. Examine the contents of the **General** tab that appears. **Used Space** and **Free Space**, together with the device's total **Capacity**, are all shown.

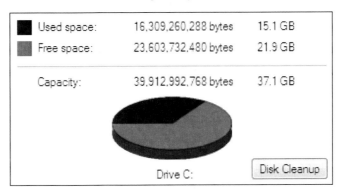

7.   Click **OK** to close the dialog box.

8.   Explore the space used, space available and total capacities of other devices connected to your computer (if applicable).

9.   When you are finished, leave the **Computer** window open for the next lesson.

Driving Lesson 55 - Accessing Storage Devices

🅿 Park and Read

All local, network and removable storage devices such as hard disk drives, memory sticks or CDs and DVDs can be accessed from **Windows Explorer**.

ℹ️ *As an example, this exercise will open your computer's built-in hard disk drive. This contains all of your computer's operating system and program files.*

🖐 Manoeuvres

1. The **Computer** window should still be open from the previous lesson. Double-click the **Local Disk (C:)** device to open it and explore its folder structure.

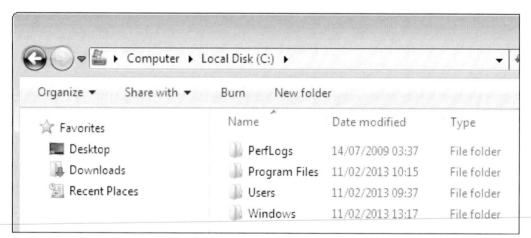

ℹ️ *If you do not have a **Local Disk (C:)**, simply choose another device.*

2. Examine the folder structure that appears in the **View Pane**. As with all devices in *Windows*, a hierarchical folder structure is used.

ℹ️ *The file and folder navigation techniques described in Section 3 can all be used to explore the contents of local and removable storage devices.*

ℹ️ *Your personal **Documents**, **Music**, **Pictures** and **Video** folders are simply subfolders of the **Users** folder. Files used by Windows are stored in the **Windows** folder and files used by your programs are stored in **Program Files**.*

3. Briefly explore the folder structure of the drive. When you are finished, select **Computer** on the **Navigation Pane** to return to the **Device List**.

ℹ️ *Although it is quite safe to view files in the **Windows** and **Program Files** folders, you must never make any changes to them. This could damage system software and prevent Windows from working correctly.*

Driving Lesson 56 - Adding Storage Devices

▣ Park and Read

As you learned in *Section 1*, connecting peripherals such as USB storage devices and memory cards is usually a case of "plug and play". Your computer will immediately notice that a peripheral has been connected and will automatically install the software needed to use it.

i *You will need a removable storage device such as a USB memory stick or flash memory card in order to complete this lesson. If one is not available, don't worry – simply read the **Manoeuvres** for information.*

⇗ Manoeuvres

1.   The **Computer** window should still be open from the previous lesson. If you have a USB memory stick or similar device, connect it to your computer now. After a moment, an entry for it – similar to that shown below – will appear in the **Device List**.

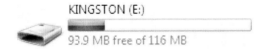

KINGSTON (E:)
93.9 MB free of 116 MB

i *Many different types of digital device have storage space that can be accessed via* Windows. *For example, digital cameras require space for photos, media players require space for music and videos, and modern smart phones require space for photos, music, videos, games and more.*

2.   Double-click the newly connected storage device to open it and explore its contents. Alternatively, click it once on the **Navigation Pane**.

i *Using the cut, copy and paste techniques described in Section 3, files and folders can be copied to and from removable storage devices.*

3.   Practice copying files and folders from the **Computer Essentials** folder to your removable storage device (and vice versa).

i *By default, files and folders dragged between different devices are copied, not moved.*

i *If a computer is connected to a network, it is also easy to access, cut, copy and paste files and folders located on other computers.*

4.   When you are finished, delete any files and folders copied during this lesson. Notice that they are not moved to the **Recycle Bin**.

Driving Lesson 56 - Continued

5.   Select **Computer** on the **Navigation Pane** to return to the **Device List**.

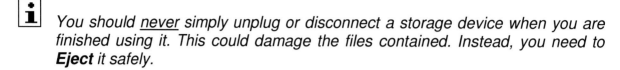 *You should never simply unplug or disconnect a storage device when you are finished using it. This could damage the files contained. Instead, you need to Eject it safely.*

6.   Right-click your storage device to display a pop-up menu. From the options that appear, select **Eject**.

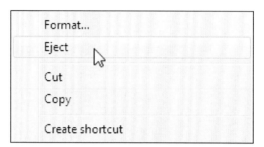

7.   After a moment, the device will be removed from the device list and a message will appear on the **Taskbar**.

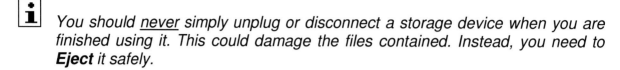 *An alternative way to safely eject a device is to click the **Safely Remove Hardware and Eject Media** button, , that appears in the **Notification Area** whenever a removable storage medium is connected.*

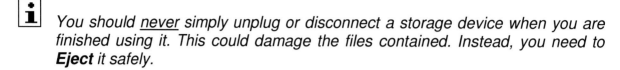 *If a message appears informing you that the device cannot be removed as it is in use, simply close all **Windows Explorer** windows and try again. If any programs are/were using files on the device, these should be closed too.*

8.   It is now safe for you to remove your device. Please do so now.

9.   Close all windows and return to the **Desktop**.

Driving Lesson 57 - Compressing Files

Park and Read

To reduce the space occupied by older files and folders that you no longer use but wish to keep, you can create **compressed** versions of them. This process is known as **zipping** and shrinks files down to a fraction of their original size.

Furthermore, as it is becoming more and more popular to store or share files online or via e-mail, zipping also allows you to package files and folders together into one smaller file. This technique makes it much easier and quicker to send and receive multiple files at once.

Windows 7 has file compression and decompression features built in. Other operating systems and earlier versions of Windows may require the installation of a separate program to handle such files.

Manoeuvres

1. Open the **Documents** library and navigate to the **Computer Essentials** data files folder.

2. The **Databases** folder currently contains two files. To "zip" this folder and all of its contents, right click on it and select **Send to | Compressed (zipped) folder**.

3. After a moment the zip file **Databases** appears containing a compressed *copy* of the **Databases** folder. Press <**Enter**> to confirm the default zip file's name (which is the same as the original folder name).

*A zipped folder is actually a file like any other. It has a **.zip** extension. That is why a zipped folder and a normal folder can share the same name.*

4. Using the **Organize** button, view the properties for the **Databases** zip file. Notice that it has a file size of nearly 55 KB.

File sizes are commonly measured in Bytes (B), KiloBytes (KB), MegaBytes (MB), GigaBytes (GB) and TeraBytes (TB). There are 1024 Bytes in a KiloByte, 1024 KiloByes in a MegaByte, 1024 MegaBytes in a GigaByte, and so on. Please refer to Driving Lesson 7 for more details.

5. Similarly, view the properties for the **Databases** folder. This has a total file size of 912 KB.

The zip file has reduced the folder and its contents by almost 95%.

Driving Lesson 57 - Continued

ℹ️ *The amount that a file can be reduced when zipped depends on its size and type. Some files can be compressed a lot, others only a little.*

6. Open the **Publications** folder and locate the file **Renaissance**. To zip this single file only, right click on it and again select **Send to | Compressed (zipped) folder**.

7. After a moment the zip file **Renaissance** appears containing a compressed *copy* of the **Renaissance** publication. Press <**Enter**> to confirm the file name.

ℹ️ *Notice that the file size of the zip is less than half that of the original file.*

8. Select the files **Company News** and **HS Guidelines** *together*. Then, right click on either one and again select **Send to | Compressed (zipped) folder**.

9. Rename the new zip file **Compressed Files** and press <**Enter**>. Again, notice that the size of the zip is less than the combined total of the two original files.

Documents library Publications			Arrange by:
Name	Date modified	Type	Size
Company News.docx	13/02/2013 12:03	Microsoft Word Document	19 KB
Compressed Files.zip	22/02/2013 13:58	Compressed (zipped) Folder	29 KB
HS Guidelines.docx	12/02/2013 09:09	Microsoft Word Document	17 KB
Renaissance.pub	26/01/2011 11:57	Microsoft Publisher Document	98 KB
Renaissance.zip	22/02/2013 13:54	Compressed (zipped) Folder	36 KB

ℹ️ *Dragging and dropping files and folders onto an existing zip will add copies of them to the file.*

10. Return to the **Computer Essentials** folder and leave it open for the next lesson.

Driving Lesson 58 - Extracting Files

▣ Park and Read

Before the compressed contents of a zip file can be used, it is advisable to **extract** them. This is because it is not possible to edit files contained in a zip.

⮑ Manoeuvres

1. With the **Computer Essentials** data files window open from the previous lesson, click once on the file **Meeting**. Notice the compressed (zipped) icon in the **Details Pane**.

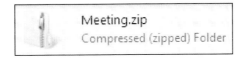

Meeting.zip
Compressed (zipped) Folder

2. Next, double-click the **Meeting** zip file to open it and view the contents.

i *Items can be removed from a zip file by simply selected and deleting them.*

i *Even though Windows appears to treat zip files as a normal folder, it is generally not possible to save changes made to the files within. For this reason, it is recommended that you extract the files first.*

3. Return to the **Computer Essentials** folder. Then, right click the **Meetings** zip file and, from the options displayed, select **Extract All**. The **Extract Compressed (Zipped) Folders** dialog box appears.

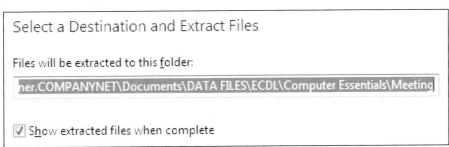

Select a Destination and Extract Files

Files will be extracted to this folder:

ner.COMPANYNET\Documents\DATA FILES\ECDL\Computer Essentials\Meeting

☑ Show extracted files when complete

i *The folder path shown matches the location of the zipped file.*

4. Remove the tick from the **Show extracted files when complete** checkbox (which simply opens the extracted contents in a new window).

5. Click **Extract**. After a moment the zipped files will be extracted and the dialog box will close automatically. Notice that a new folder, **Meeting**, has now appeared in the **Computer Essentials** folder.

6. Open the **Meeting** folder to reveal 4 normal, uncompressed files. You can edit and work with these files as you would any other.

7. Close any open windows and return to the **Desktop**.

Driving Lesson 59 - Revision

P Park and Read

At the end of every section you get the chance to complete one or more revision exercises to develop your skills and prepare you for your ECDL certification test. You should aim to complete the following steps without referring back to the previous lessons.

Manoeuvres

1. How much space is currently used on your computer's **Local Disk (C:)**? How much space is still available?

2. Open your **Documents** library and navigate to the **Computer Essentials** data files folder.

3. Examine the properties of the **Presentations** folder and determine its size.

4. Compress the **Presentations** folder to create a new zip file named **Presentations.zip**.

5. Examine the properties of the **Presentations** zip file and determine its size. Notice the space that has been saved!

6. Delete the original **Presentations** folder and all of its contents.

7. Next, open the **Reports** folder to reveal three files.

8. Compress the **Budget Report** document, confirming the new zip file's default name.

9. Then, compress the files **Accounts** and **Financial Report**. Name the zip file **Finances**.

10. Rename the zip **Budget Report** as **Annual Summary**.

i *Hint: you can rename a zip file just as you would any other type of file.*

11. Return to the **Computer Essentials** folder.

12. Finally, extract all of the files stored in the **Presentations** zip file.

13. Delete the **Presentations** _zip_ file, leaving the uncompressed **Presentations** folder remaining.

14. Close any open windows, returning to your **Desktop**.

i *Now complete the **Record of Achievement Matrix** at the back of the guide. You should only move on when confident with the topics and features described in this section.*

Section 7
Control Panel

By the end of this section you should be able to:

Open and use the Control Panel

View system, firewall and network information

Change date and time

Alter display settings and screen resolution

Adjust volume settings

Use different language settings

Update Windows and backup files

Install and uninstall programs

Work through the **Driving Lessons** in this section to gain an understanding of the above features.

For each **Driving Lesson**, read all of the **Park and Read** instructions and then perform the numbered steps of the **Manoeuvres**. Complete the **Revision** exercise(s) at the end of the section to test your knowledge.

Driving Lesson 60 - Control Panel

▣ Park and Read

The *Windows* **Control Panel** contains tools that control how the *Windows* environment looks and performs. For example, the sound volume, screen resolution, date, time and background picture can all be changed from here.

Any changes made on the **Control Panel** are saved until changed again, and any changes made will still be in effect after closing and restarting *Windows*.

⌐ Manoeuvres

1. Click the **Start** button and, from the list on the right, select **Control Panel**.

2. The **Control Panel** window opens. Notice that the various settings are grouped under related headings.

> **ℹ** *If the* **Control Panel** *does not appear as shown above, make sure that* **Category** *is selected in the* **View by** *drop-down list.*

3. Maximise the window and then examine the various options available on this screen. These are described in more detail below.

Category	Features
System and Security	Adjust your computer's security settings, back-up files, change power options and update your software.

Driving Lesson 60 - Continued

Network and Internet	Share files and change how your computer connects to a local network or the Internet.
Hardware and Sound	Add, remove and configure the hardware attached to your computer including storage devices, mice, printers, and display and sound devices.
Programs	Manage the programs that are installed on your computer, or remove them altogether.
User Accounts	Add or remove computer users and change account details, security levels and passwords.
Appearance and Personalisation	Change the way *Windows* looks, from desktop backgrounds to text colours and sizes.
Clock, Language and Region	Change your computer's date and time, and alter regional settings such as language and currency.
Ease of Access	Useful settings to allow you to more easily access your computer if you are vision, hearing or mobility impaired.

i *You can place your mouse pointer over a category title for a more detailed* ***ToolTip***.

i *Depending on your* ***User Account*** *type (accessible via* ***User Accounts***), *you may be restricted from making significant changes to your computer. As a rule, if you are connected to a network, only the person in charge of that network (known as the system* ***Administrator***) *is allowed to make changes to a computer that affect other users.*

i *If a computer setting can only be changed by an* ***Administrator***, *a* ***User Account Control*** *icon,* 🛡, *will appear on the button or option that applies those changes.*

4. Leave the **Control Panel** open. In the following lessons you will explore some of the categories described above in more detail.

Driving Lesson 61 - System Information

▣ Park and Read

The **Control Panel** can be used to view important information about a computer system. Details include the computer's name, processor speed, memory capacity, and the version of *Windows* that is installed.

ℹ️ *System information is useful to know when buying and installing new hardware or software. Not all devices and programs are compatible with each other and most have specific* **minimum requirements**. *For example, programs may only work on a specific version of* Windows *or on a computer with a minimum amount of memory.*

👉 Manoeuvres

1.   With the **Control Panel** open, click once on **System and Security**.

2.   A second list of system settings is displayed. Select **System** to display basic information about your computer system.

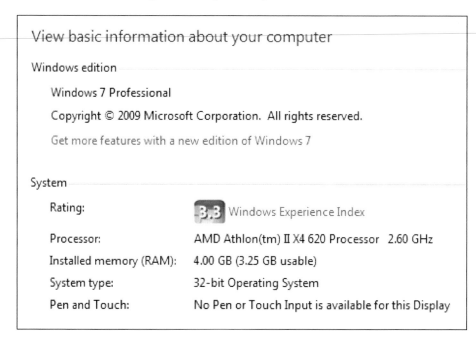

ℹ️ *As computers can be built using a combination of different components, your computer's basic information will appear differently to that shown above.*

Driving Lesson 61 - Continued

3.   Examine the information that appears. In particular, notice the **Windows edition** information (which shows the operating system's name and version number).

4.   Also locate the **Processor** type and speed, the amount of **Installed memory (RAM)**, and the **Computer name**.

> **i** *Advanced system settings can also be accessed from the **Navigation Pane**.*

5.   Return to the **Control Panel's** main starting screen by clicking **Control Panel Home** (located on the window's **Navigation Pane**).

> **i** *Alternatively, you can use the **Back** button.*

6.   Leave the **Control Panel** open for the next lesson.

Driving Lesson 62 - Display Settings

▣ Park and Read

The display quality of the information that you see on your computer screen – words, pictures, videos – is directly affected by your screen's **resolution**. The higher the resolution the more crisp and clear your display becomes but the smaller everything appears. *Windows* will usually choose the best screen resolution for you automatically, but if you find this uncomfortable to work with you can manually choose a more appropriate setting.

↱ Manoeuvres

1.   With the **Control Panel** open, click once on **Appearance and Personalization**.

2.   Examine the various options that appear to see what changes are possible.

3.   Click once on **Display**. Read the description of this setting and click on each of the three size options in turn to see a small preview. Selecting **Medium** or **Larger** would increase *Windows'* font and icon sizes.

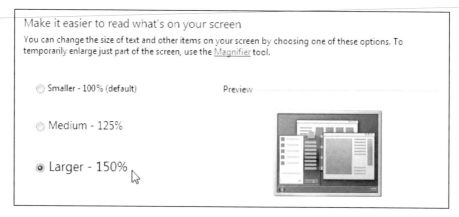

ℹ️ *Do not click **Apply** to adjust font and icon settings now as you will be required to log off for the changes to take effect.*

4.   From the **Navigation Pane** on the left, select **Adjust resolution**. From here it is possible to change the screen's resolution.

ℹ️ *A popular screen resolution in business is 1366x768. This creates a picture with 1366 **pixels** – or single coloured dots – displayed across and 768 down the screen (creating a grid of 1049088 pixels).*

Driving Lesson 62 - Continued

5. Drop down the **Resolution** box and examine the various screen resolutions available. Make a note of your current resolution.

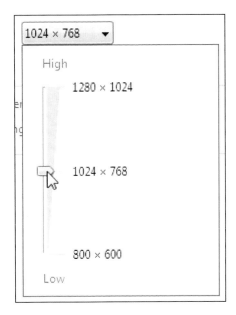

6. Then, use the slider to select a new setting and click the **Apply** button. Your screen may go dark or flicker for a moment – this is perfectly normal.

7. Observe the effect. Wait a moment and your screen will <u>automatically</u> **Revert** to its previous setting. <u>Do not</u> choose to **Keep changes**.

    In practice you can choose whichever screen resolution you feel is most practical and comfortable. However, for the remainder of this guide, it is recommended that you leave your screen resolution at its original setting.

8. Click **Cancel**. Then, click once on **Appearance and Personalization** on the **Address Bar** to return directly to that screen.

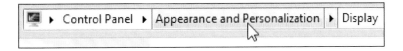

9. Next, select **Personalization**. Your computer's **Desktop Background** picture, **Window Color** and **Screen Saver** can all be changed here.

    Window Color *allows you to fine tune the various colours and fonts used by each window, from title bar and border colours to font types and sizes. However, these are best set using **themes**, as you will see later.*

    *A **screen saver** is a moving pattern or message that appears on the screen after a set period of inactivity. Originally this was used to prevent damage to a computer screen but, with today's technology, this is rarely a problem.*

10. Select the **Desktop Background** icon in the **Personalization** window.

Driving Lesson 62 - Continued

11.   Drop down the list of **Picture location** folders and select some to see the images available. Finally, select **Windows Desktop Backgrounds**.

i *By selecting **Pictures Library** you can view and select custom images stored in your own **Pictures** library folders.*

12.   Click once to select any picture that you like. Then, minimise the **Control Panel** window to see the effect.

13.   Restore the **Control Panel** and experiment with different images.

i *Notice the **Picture position** drop-down box. This can be used to adjust the size, scaling and position of the chosen background image.*

14.   Click **Cancel** to leave the background image unchanged and return to the **Personalization** window.

i *The large box on the **Personalization** screen allows you to select different themes. These are pre-set combinations of **Desktop Background**, **Windows Color** and **Sounds**.*

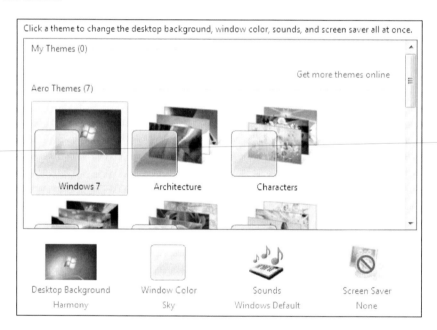

15.   Examine the contents of the **Themes** box and make a note of the one that is currently selected. Then, select other themes and observe the effect. Notice that new **Desktop Backgrounds**, **Window Colors** and **Sounds** are selected (minimise the **Control Panel** to see **Desktop** changes).

16.   When you are finished, restore your default theme.

17.   Return to the main starting screen by clicking **Control Panel Home**.

i *Display settings can also be altered by right clicking the **Desktop** and selecting **Screen Resolution** or **Personalize** from the shortcut menu that appears.*

Driving Lesson 63 - Sound Settings

▣ Park and Read

Sound settings in *Windows* are grouped into two main categories: **Playback** and **Recording**. Playback controls how sounds are made by your computer; recording controls how sounds are captured by your computer.

↱ Manoeuvres

1. With the **Control Panel** open, click once on **Hardware and Sound**. Examine the various options that appear to see what changes are possible, and then select **Sound**.

2. The **Sound** dialog box opens. Display each of the tabs (**Playback**, **Recording**, **Sounds** and **Communications**) and explore the various options available.

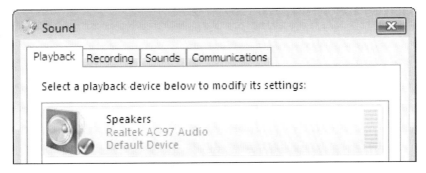

ⓘ *Notice that custom sounds can also be assigned to events in* Windows *using the **Sounds** tab. These sounds are set when a theme is chosen on the **Personalize** screen of the **Control Panel**.*

3. Return to the **Playback** tab. If applicable, the default device inside your computer used for playing sound is displayed with a tick symbol, ✅.

4. Select this default device (or another, if no default device is available) and click the **Properties** button, ⎡ Properties ⎤.

5. On the **Speakers Properties** dialog box display the **Levels** tab. You can adjust your computer's playback volume here.

6. Click **Cancel** to return to the **Sound** dialog box without making changes.

ⓘ *An icon to adjust sound volume may also be available in the **Notification Area** on the **Taskbar**.*

Driving Lesson 63 - Continued

7. Locate and click the sound volume icon, 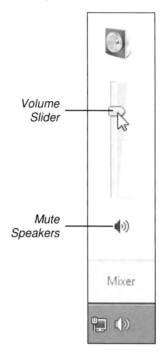, in the **Notification Area**. A volume slider control will appear.

8. Click and drag the slider up and down to vary the sound level.

Volume
Slider

Mute
Speakers

Mixer

9. Click the **Mute Speakers** button, ◀», to switch off the sound completely.

10. Click the **Mute Speakers** button again to restore the previous playback level.

11. Return the volume to a low level (to avoid being surprised by a loud noise next time a sound is played).

i   *Most applications that play sounds will also have their own built-in volume controls (e.g. **Windows Media Player**, as shown below). Speakers can also have their own volume control dials.*

Volume
Slider

12. Next, return to the **Sound** dialog box and display the **Recording** tab. If one exists, view the **Properties** of your default recording device.

13. Explore the settings available, and then click **Cancel** to return to the **Sound** dialog box without making changes.

14. Click **Cancel** again to close the **Sound** dialog box.

15. Finally, return to the **Control Panel's** main starting screen by clicking **Control Panel Home**.

Driving Lesson 64 - Date and Time Settings

▣ Park and Read

Every computer has a built-in clock that *Windows* uses to find the date and time.

> **i** Windows *will automatically adjust the time to take into account daylight savings.*

⤷ Manoeuvres

1. With the **Control Panel** open, click once on **Clock, Language, and Region**. Then, select **Date and Time** to display the **Date and Time** dialog box.

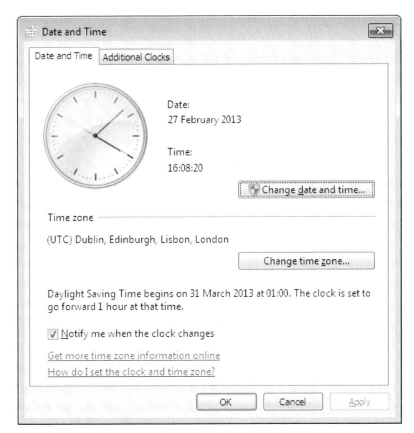

> **i** *Alternatively, click the time and date shown in the **Notification Area** on the **Taskbar** and select **Change date and time settings**.*

2. Examine the contents of the dialog box. Then, click **Change date and time**.

> **i** *Depending on how your computer is set up, you may be restricted from changing the date and time as this will affect other users. In general, only an **Administrator** is able to make system-wide changes such as this.*

Driving Lesson 64 - Continued

3.   If you are prompted to enter an **Administrator** password, click **No**. However, if you have permission, the **Date and Time Settings** dialog box will appear.

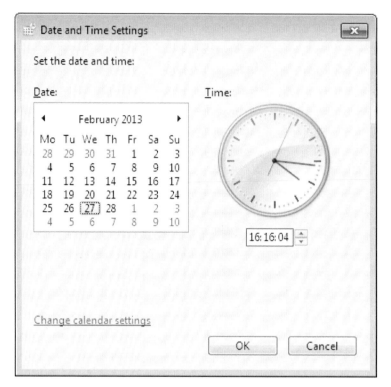

ℹ️ *The current **Date** can be selected on the calendar and the time changed by editing the value in the **Time** box.*

4.   If the **Date and Time Settings** dialog box is open, click **Cancel** to close it without making changes.

ℹ️ *When travelling, you are able to select different time zones without needing to be an **Administrator**.*

5.   Click **Change time zone** to display the **Time Zone Settings** dialog box.

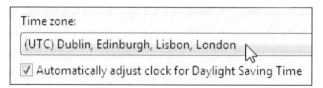

6.   Click the **Time zone** drop-down and briefly examine the various time zones available. Click the **Time zone** button again to close the list.

ℹ️ *Settings to control automatic daylight savings can also be found here.*

7.   Click **Cancel** to close the dialog box without making changes. Then, click **Cancel** again to close the **Date and Time** dialog box.

Driving Lesson 65 - Language Settings

▣ Park and Read

You can add new **input languages** in *Windows* so that you can enter and edit text in multiple languages. This is particularly useful for people who work with documents in languages other that the computer's default.

You can also change how *Windows* **formats** information such as dates, times, measurements and currency.

⌒ Manoeuvres

1. With the **Control Panel** open on the **Clock, Language, and Region** screen, select **Region and Language**.

2. The **Region and Language** dialog box appears. Briefly examine the contents of all four tabs to see the settings that can be changed.

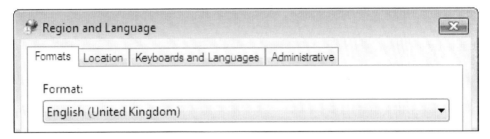

3. Return to the **Formats** tab. The settings here control how properties such as date and time are shown in *Windows*. The default values are set based on the country or region selected in the **Format** drop-down box.

ⓘ *Formatting options for properties such as numbers, measurements and currency can also be accessed by clicking the **Additional settings** button.*

ⓘ *In practice, you can select the country or region from the **Format** drop-down that best matches your own circumstances. However, for the remainder of this guide, it is recommended that you continue to use the default setting.*

4. Select the **Keyboards and Languages** tab and click the **Change keyboards** button. The settings here allow you to add, remove and manage multiple input languages.

5. Click the **Add** button to see a list of all available input languages. For demonstration purposes, locate and expand **Arabic (Algeria)**.

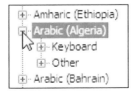

Driving Lesson 65 - Continued

6.   Next, expand **Keyboard** and place a tick in the **Arabic (102) AZERTY** checkbox.

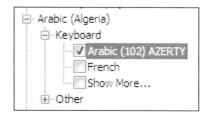

[i]   *If **Arabic (102) AZERTY** is already selected or cannot be found, simply find and choose another language and keyboard layout.*

7.   Click the **Preview** button to see how each key on your keyboard will "map" to Arabic characters when pressed.

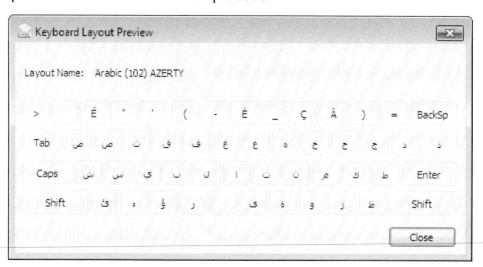

8.   Click **Close** to close the preview, and then click **OK** to add the new input language to *Windows*. Notice it appears in the **Installed services** box, ready to be used.

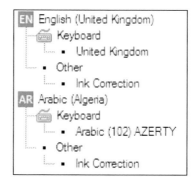

[i]   *The <u>default</u> input language can be chosen by selecting one of the **Installed services** in the **Default input language** drop-down box.*

9.   Click **OK**. Notice the **Language Bar** button in the **Notification Area,** EN.

10.   Click the **Language Bar** button and select **Show the Language bar**.

Driving Lesson 65 - Continued

11. The **Language Bar** appears at the top of the screen. This will remain on the screen and on top of all other windows until closed.

 *When a new language is added, the **Language Bar** allows you to switch between input languages quickly and easily.*

12. Leave the **Region and Language** dialog box open and start the *WordPad* program.

13. With the cursor flashing in the top left of the **Document Window**, enter the following line:

     This is typed using my default input language.

14. Press <**Enter**>. Then, click the currently selected input language on the **Language Bar** and select **Arabic (Algeria)**.

15. Return to *WordPad* and experiment by entering text using your keyboard. Observe the effect.

 *Using the powerful **Language Bar**, you can add and use as many different languages as you need.*

16. Close the *WordPad* document <u>without</u> saving. Then, return to the **Region and Language** dialog box.

17. Click **Change keyboards** to view your available input languages again.

18. Select **Arabic (Algeria)** in the **Installed services** box and click **Remove**. The input language is removed (and the **Language Bar** will disappear).

19. Click **OK** and then **OK** again to return to the **Control Panel**.

20. Finally, return to the **Control Panel's** main starting screen by clicking **Control Panel Home**.

Driving Lesson 66 - Windows Firewall

▣ Park and Read

Windows Firewall is used to help keep a network-connected computer safe by preventing people and malicious software from remotely gaining access to it. By automatically monitoring incoming and outgoing data, it also "blocks" programs on a computer from communicating with other network-connected devices without permission.

The firewall is simply a piece of system software that automatically runs "in the background" when Windows *starts. It usually does not require your attention unless your device is connected to a new network.*

⟲ Manoeuvres

1. With the **Control Panel** open, click once on **System and Security**.

2. Examine the various options that appear to see what changes are possible, and then select **Windows Firewall**.

3. Familiarise yourself with the options available on this screen.

*Three **network locations** are shown: **Domain networks**, **Home or work (private) networks**, and **Public networks**. You will probably be connected to one of these.*

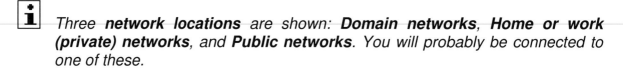

When you connect an ICT device to a new network for the <u>first</u> time, Windows *will prompt you to choose a network location for it. Depending on your choice,* Windows *will <u>automatically</u> set up, save and apply the best security settings for that type of connection.*

4. Click the expand button, ⌄, to the right of each network location to view the settings for that connection type.

5. Read the short descriptions that appear for each location (as described on the next page).

Driving Lesson 66 - Continued

Network Location	Description	Security Level
Domain networks	Networks at a workplace that are attached to a domain (a domain is the name given to a company network).	Lowest
Home or work (private) networks	Networks at home or work where you know and trust the people and devices on the network.	Medium
Public networks	Networks in public places such as airports, libraries and coffee shops.	Highest

 When you connect your Windows *device to a public network (e.g. a Wi-Fi hotspot at a café) choose* **Public networks**. *This prevents other people from accessing your computer. At home, where you may want to exchange files and share resources between devices, select* **Home or work (private) networks**.

6.   Click the **Back** button once to return to the **System and Security** screen.

Driving Lesson 67 - Windows Update

▣ Park and Read

As errors and security problems are found in *Windows* and other *Microsoft* programs, the creators release updates to fix them. It is therefore important that you download these updates to keep your computer running at its best. Luckily, **Windows Update** will do this automatically for you.

⌐ Manoeuvres

1.   With the **System and Security** screen open, click once on **Windows Update**. If your computer has all of the latest updates installed, this message will appear.

> ℹ *Keeping your computer up-to-date protects it from malware and hackers. You will learn more about this in Section 10.*

2.   *Windows* will usually check for updates automatically and install them when you shut down your computer (which you should always let it do). To check for and install updates manually, click **Check for updates** on the **Navigation Pane**. Do that now.

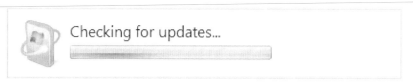

3.   Checking for updates will take a little time to complete. While *Windows* is searching, click **Change settings** on the **Navigation Pane**. Examine the settings available on this screen.

> ℹ *If you are using a public or shared computer, it is possible that only the network* ***Administrator*** *will be able to make changes here and install updates.*

4.   Click the **Back** button to return to the **Windows Update** screen. If the check has finished, there may be updates available to download and install. <u>Do not</u> do this now.

> ℹ *It can sometimes take a long time to download and install updates, and you may need to restart your computer a number of times during the process. Consider returning to this screen at the end of this section and completing the update.*

Driving Lesson 67 - Continued

5.   Click the **Back** button once to return to the **System and Security** screen. Don't worry if *Windows* is still searching for updates – it will continue to do so in the background until it is finished (a pop-up in the **Notification Area** will appear if updates are found).

ℹ️   *Different types of software have other ways of searching for and downloading updates. If a program that you trust informs you that an update is available, it is always a good idea to download and install it.*

ℹ️   *A **bug** is not the same thing as a **virus**. A bug is simply an error or fault in a piece of software that stops it working correctly. Software updates are released to fix, or "patch", bugs.*

Driving Lesson 68 - Backing Up

▣ Park and Read

Regular **backing up** is essential if you have important data stored on your computer that you cannot lose. In business, this is often done daily. At home, you may decide to backup your personal files less frequently (perhaps only once a month or so). Of course, the more regularly you backup, the less chance you have of losing recent changes and new files.

i *A lot of people put off backing up their data until it is too late. Unfortunately, hardware failure, accidental file deletion and loss/theft of ICT devices occur more often than you might think. Consider the impact of losing all of your documents, pictures and music if this was to happen to you.*

To backup your data, simply copy all of your files to a writable CD/DVD, removable storage device or cloud storage location.

i *Back-ups should always be kept in a secure, remote location (in case of fire, flood or theft where the contents of an entire building could be lost).*

If your computer suffers a hardware failure or is lost, you can use a backup to **restore** your data. This is simply a case of copying the files and folders stored in the backup back onto your (fixed or newly purchased) computer.

i *Windows has a built-in **Backup and Restore** feature which makes backing up and restoring files easy. However, this feature can only be used by an **Administrator** and so it is only briefly described here.*

⌐ Manoeuvres

1.   With the **System and Security** screen open, click once on **Backup and Restore**. Examine the options that appear.

i *There are two main types of backup built into* Windows. *You can either backup personal files and folders only or you can backup the entire computer (**Create a system image**). The first is recommended as it is the fastest and easiest.*

2.   Notice the **Set up backup** button (do not click it now). If you have permission, this allows you to create a new backup (if a backup already exists, **Change settings** can be used instead to adjust its settings).

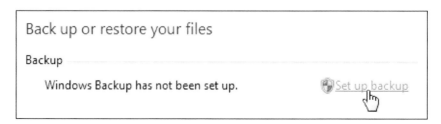

Driving Lesson 68 - Continued

i *The* Windows *backup feature prompts you to select a location to store your backup (from the list of ICT storage devices currently connected to your computer). By default, the backup will automatically include all of the files on your **Desktop** and in your library folders.*

i Windows *will schedule a backup to occur automatically at the same time each week (usually 7pm on a Sunday night). For the backup to occur, the computer must be switched on and a backup storage device connected. The backup can also be run manually at any time.*

i *To restore data, the backup device simply needs to be connected to the computer. An option to **Restore my files** will appear on the **Backup and Restore screen**.*

3. Return to the **Control Panel's** main starting screen by clicking **Control Panel Home**.

i *As routine backups often overwrite previous backup files, businesses will from time to time make a second copy of a backup on separate ICT storage media. This is never overwritten and provides a "snapshot" of data that can be returned to at a later date (if needed). These special types of backup are called **archives**.*

Driving Lesson 69 - Installing Programs

▣ Park and Read

To add a new program to your computer it must first be **installed**. To do this, a small utility packaged with the program copies all of the necessary files to the correct folders, "registers" the program with *Windows*, and finally creates **Start Menu** entries.

i *An installation utility is also a program (often called **Setup.exe** or **Install.exe**).*

If you are installing a program from a CD or DVD, the installation utility will usually run automatically when the disc is inserted into your computer (you may first be prompted to run the setup program). If it does not, instructions that come with the disc will usually indicate how to start the installation.

i *You can open and explore the contents of the disc by clicking **Open folder to view files**. Alternatively, use the **Computer** view to navigate the disc's folder structure.*

i *Most Windows installation utilities use a simple **setup wizard** – a sequence of dialog boxes – that guide you through the installation process. Simply follow their on-screen instructions to complete the installation.*

If the program was obtained via the Internet, you will need to run it manually by double-clicking the downloaded file. Executable files are often zipped to reduce their file size and download times and will need to be extracted first.

i *As you will learn later, it is very important to be aware of viruses and other malicious software when downloading and running files from the Internet.*

i *In general, only a computer's **Administrator** is able to install new programs. On a business network, they are often able to do this remotely.*

Driving Lesson 70 - Uninstalling Programs

🄿 Park and Read

Unwanted programs can be removed from your computer by **uninstalling** them. This will delete the program completely and free up any storage space used.

Note that any files created using the program (e.g. documents, spreadsheets, presentations, publications, databases) will *not* be deleted.

ℹ️ *Manually deleting program files and folders will not remove an application correctly and may damage* Windows.

Manoeuvres

1.   With the **Control Panel** open, click once on **Programs**.

2.   Examine the various options that appear to see what changes are possible, and then select **Programs and Features**.

3.   A list of all of the programs that are currently installed on your computer is displayed. Examine the list and notice that the program's **Name**, **Publisher**, **Version**, date **Installed On** and **Size** are all shown.

ℹ️ *The* ***Size*** *of the program refers to know much storage space it occupies.*

4.   Select any one item and notice the options that appear on the **Toolbar** above the list.

Organize ▾   Uninstall   Change   Repair

ℹ️ *Depending on the item selected,* ***Change*** *or* ***Repair*** *may not appear.*

5.   Locate the **Uninstall** button (<u>do not</u> click it). This can be used to permanently remove the selected program from your computer. The program will also be removed from your **Start Menu**.

ℹ️ *If you experience any problems starting and using a program, the* ***Repair*** *option (if present) can be used instead to reinstall the program and fix any issues.*

6.   Close the **Control Panel** and return to your **Desktop**.

ℹ️ *Shortcuts to uninstall a program may also appear on the* ***Start Menu*** *(usually in the program's folder).*

Driving Lesson 71 - Revision

▣ Park and Read

At the end of every section you get the chance to complete one or more revision exercises to develop your skills and prepare you for your ECDL certification test. You should aim to complete the following steps without referring back to the previous lessons.

↱ Manoeuvres

1. Using the **Control Panel**, find out the version of *Windows* that is installed and how much memory (RAM) your computer has.

2. Change your **Desktop** picture to another of your choosing. View your **Desktop** to see the effect.

3. What is your current screen resolution?

4. Select the **Windows 7** theme to restore default settings.

5. Add two new additional languages and keyboard layouts of your own choosing (for example, try *Bengali* and *Russian*).

6. Using the **Language Bar**, experiment with typing text into *WordPad* using different languages.

7. When you are finished, close *WordPad* without saving changes.

8. Remove the two new additional languages added in step 5.

9. What is the current status of the **Windows Firewall**?

10. View the programs that are currently installed on your computer. How much space does the largest program occupy?

11. Check for *Windows* updates.

12. If you are listening to music on your computer, name three possible ways to control the volume.

13. Why should you back-up your computer and its data?

14. Close any open windows and programs and return to your **Desktop**.

ℹ️ *Sample answers can be found at the back of the guide.*

ℹ️ *Now complete the **Record of Achievement Matrix** at the back of the guide. You should only move on when confident with the topics and features described in this section.*

Section 8
Printers

By the end of this section you should be able to:

View a list of installed printers

Install and uninstall a printer

Print a test page

Set a default printer

Work with print jobs

Work through the **Driving Lessons** in this section to gain an understanding of the above features.

For each **Driving Lesson**, read all of the **Park and Read** instructions and then perform the numbered steps of the **Manoeuvres**. Complete the **Revision** exercise(s) at the end of the section to test your knowledge.

Driving Lesson 72 - Printing

Park and Read

Printers are a great way to produce hard copies of information stored in digital format. Using *Windows*, it is easy to find, manage and use peripheral printer devices that are connected directly to your own computer or to computers elsewhere on a network.

A properties dialog box can be displayed for each available printer allowing various print settings to be changed. If more than one printer is installed, it is possible to select a **default**.

i *The following lessons assume you have at least one printer installed on your computer. If you do not, simply read the **Manoeuvres** for information.*

Manoeuvres

1. Open the **Start Menu**. Then, select **Devices and Printers** to view a list of peripheral devices connected to your computer.

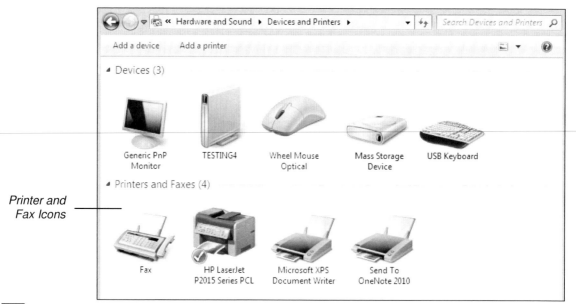

Printer and Fax Icons

i ***Devices and Printers** can also be accessed from the **Control Panel**. Your view will show a different set of device and printer icons.*

2. Locate the **Printer and Faxes** list. Any and all printers available to you can be seen here.

i *Your default printer, if you have one, is shown with a tick icon, 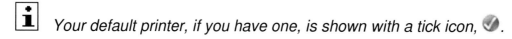.*

3. Click once on any printer to select it. Notice that a number of additional options specific to that printer now appear on the **Toolbar**.

Driving Lesson 72 - Continued

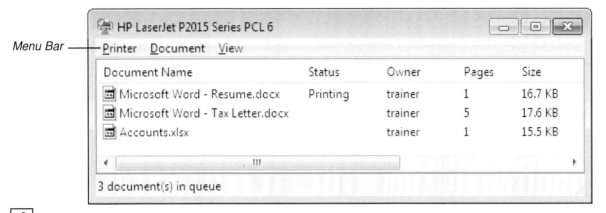 *The default printer is the printer used when printing from a program. To choose a different printer as the default, right-click its icon and select **Set as default printer**.*

4.   Click **See what's printing**. A window appears which lists all "print jobs" that are currently waiting to be printed on this printer (it is likely to be empty). This is known as a "**print queue**".

Menu Bar ────

Document Name	Status	Owner	Pages	Size
Microsoft Word - Resume.docx	Printing	trainer	1	16.7 KB
Microsoft Word - Tax Letter.docx		trainer	5	17.6 KB
Accounts.xlsx		trainer	1	15.5 KB

HP LaserJet P2015 Series PCL 6
Printer   Document   View

3 document(s) in queue

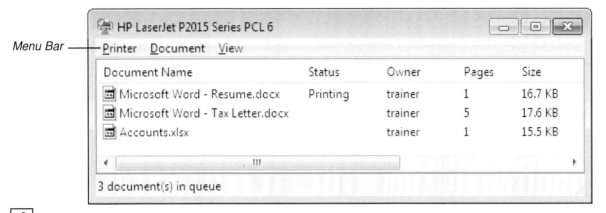 *Selected print jobs in a printer's queue can be **Paused**, **Restarted** or **Cancelled** using the **Document** menu. If a paper jam occurs on the printer or an error occurs, these settings can be used to stop and restart the print after you have resolved the problem.*

5.   Click **Document** on the **Menu Bar** to view options for managing print jobs.

6.   Close the printer queue window by clicking the **Close** button, ▣.

7.   To adjust the default settings for a printer, right click on the printer icon and select **Printing preferences** from the shortcut menu.

8.   Click each of the tabs at the top of the dialog box that appears to see which aspects of the printer's operation can be changed.

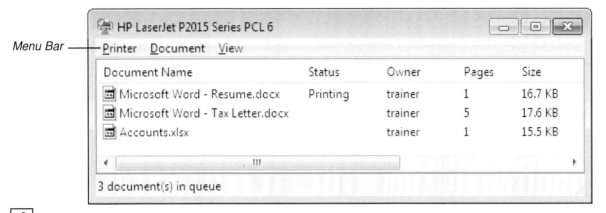 *Many of the settings shown are specific to the selected printer. Each type of printer has its own printing preferences.*

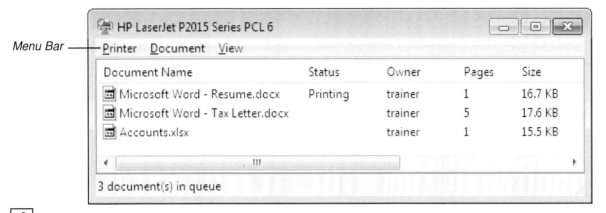 *To change a printer's name, view advanced settings or share the device with others on a network, right-click the printer icon and select **Printer properties**.*

9.   When you are finished, click **Cancel** to close the dialog box without making any changes.

10.   Leave the **Device and Printers** screen open for the next lesson.

Driving Lesson 73 - Printing a Test Page

▣ Park and Read

To check that an installed printer is working and that your computer is correctly set up to use it, a single A4 **Test Page** can be printed.

i *The information printed on a **Test Page** contains useful details about the selected printer.*

↰ Manoeuvres

1.   With the **Device and Printers** screen open, right-click on any printer and select **Printer properties**. The **Properties** dialog box appears.

i *Make sure you select a printer that is available and turned on. Printers that are unavailable appear "ghosted" in the **Devices and Printers** view.*

2.   Locate and click the **Print Test Page** button, ⌐ Print Test Page ¬, at the bottom of the **General** tab.

3.   A **Test Page** is automatically sent to the printer. Read the message that appears.

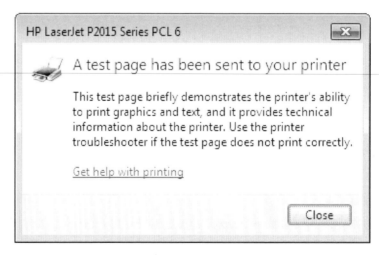

4.   Click **Close** to dismiss the message. Then, take a look at the **Test Page** that was printed.

i *Think before you print! Unnecessary printing is a waste of resources and money.*

5.   Click **OK** to close the **Properties** dialog box.

6.   Leave the **Device and Printers** screen open for the next lesson

Driving Lesson 74 - Adding a Printer

⊞ Park and Read

It is easy to add a new printer to your computer. Clicking **Add a printer** starts the **Add Printer** wizard which guides you through the process.

 When connecting a new printer directly to your computer via USB, Windows will detect the device and automatically install the software required to use it. However, it is important that you read and follow the manufacturer's instructions before connecting the device (many printers come with advanced software for managing and maintaining the printer that must to be installed first).

⌒ Manoeuvres

1. With the **Device and Printers** screen open, click **Add a printer** on the **Toolbar**. The **Add Printer** wizard starts.

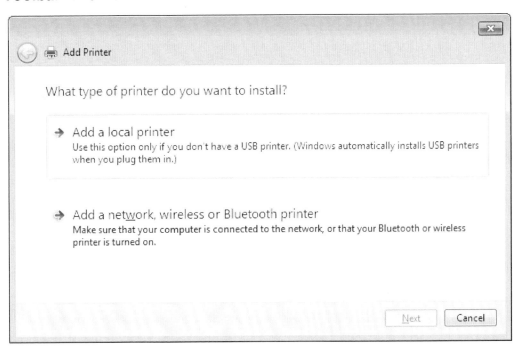

2. Examine the two options available. The first is rarely used as *Windows* automatically detects and installs a local printer when connected. However, the second option is very useful for finding and adding wireless or network printers.

 The printer, or networked computer it is connected to (if applicable), needs to be turned on to appear in the list of available printers.

3. For demonstration purposes, select **Add a network, wireless or Bluetooth printer**. *Windows* will automatically scan the network it is connecting to for available, shared printers.

Driving Lesson 74 - Continued

4. *Windows* will display details of all available printers that it can find. Don't worry if none appear in your list; simply read the following steps for information

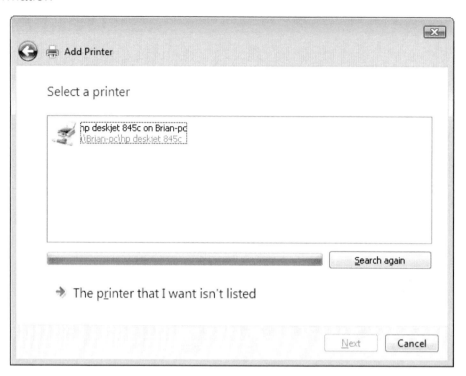

[i] *To add a printer to your **Printer and Faxes List**, simply select it and click **Next**. Windows will connect to the printer and automatically download any software required to use it (you may need to be an **Administrator** to do this). A new icon will appear in the **Printer and Faxes List** and you will be prompted to set the printer as your default printer and/or print a **Test Page**.*

[i] *Password authorisation may be required to access private printers on a network.*

5. Click **The printer that I want isn't listed**. This screen can be used to manually browse through network devices to locate a printer.

6. Click **Cancel** to return to the **Devices and Printers** window.

[i] *If you would like to install a printer that was found in step 4, feel free to do so now by launching the **Add Printer** wizard again.*

[i] *To remove a printer from the **Printer and Faxes List**, simply select it and click **Remove device** from the **Toolbar**. You can always reconnect to and add the printer again later.*

7. Close the **Devices and Printers** window.

Driving Lesson 75 - Revision

▣ Park and Read

At the end of every section you get the chance to complete one or more revision exercises to develop your skills and prepare you for your ECDL certification test. You should aim to complete the following steps without referring back to the previous lessons.

↱ Manoeuvres

1. Open the **Devices and Printers** window.

2. Select a printer to use in this revision lesson. It can be your default printer or the printer nearest to your location.

3. Print a **Test Page**.

4. View the print queue for the selected printer. How can a print job that has failed to print be removed from the queue?

5. Leave the print queue window open and start *WordPad*. In the empty document that appears, enter the following text:

   This document was printed from WordPad.

6. Print the document on your selected printer.

ℹ *Watch as the print job appears momentarily in the print queue window.*

7. Close *WordPad* without saving changes to the document.

8. Close the print queue window.

9. How do you change the default printer?

10. Use the **Windows Help and Support** feature to find information about printers. In particular, find a topic about checking or changing ink and toner cartridges.

11. Use the **Print** button, 🖨, to print a copy of the article using your selected printer.

12. Close **Windows Help and Support**. Then, close any open windows and programs and return to the **Desktop**.

ℹ *Sample answers can be found at the back of the guide.*

ℹ *Now complete the **Record of Achievement Matrix** at the back of the guide. You should only move on when confident with the topics and features described in this section.*

Section 9
Network Concepts

By the end of this section you should be able to:

Understand the purpose of a network

Recognise the main uses of a network

Connect to the Internet

Choose an ISP and connection type

Understand and recognise Wi-Fi

Identify online communication technologies

Work through the **Driving Lessons** in this section to gain an understanding of the above features.

For each **Driving Lesson**, read all of the **Park and Read** instructions and then perform the numbered steps of the **Manoeuvres**. Complete the **Revision** exercise(s) at the end of the section to test your knowledge.

Driving Lesson 76 - Networks

▣ Park and Read

A **network** is the name given to two or more ICT devices that are connected to each other. Once connected, devices on the network can safely and securely share data and resources (such as files, printers and storage devices).

Setting up a home or office network, often referred to as a **Local Area Network** (**LAN**), is very simple. All that is needed is a **router** to control the flow of data between devices and a **modem** to access the Internet. ICT devices connect to the network via the router using cables or wireless Wi-Fi connections.

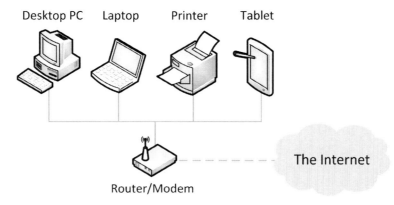

ℹ️ *These days, most routers have a built-in modem and wireless functionality.*

For larger business networks, a **server** is sometimes used. This is a dedicated computer which looks after the security of the network, manages shared services (such as Internet access and e-mail), and stores shared files.

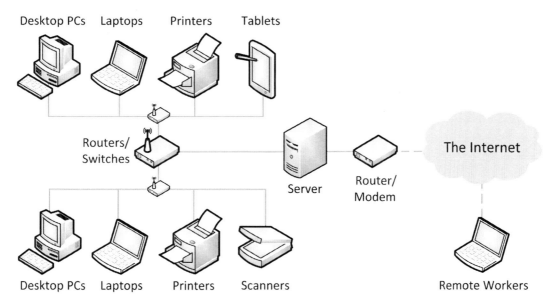

Although a network can be expensive to set up in terms of time and hardware costs, the benefits they offer often save money in the long run. For example, you can exchange data more securely and share costly resources such as printers and Internet connections.

Driving Lesson 77 - The Internet

▣ Park and Read

The **Internet**, or net for short, is a global network of linked ICT devices that allow people from all over the world to communicate and share information. Many different types of devices are able to connect to the Internet, from desktop and laptop computers to mobile phones and printers. By connecting to the Internet, both you and your equipment are able to interact with and benefit from the many features and services that it offers.

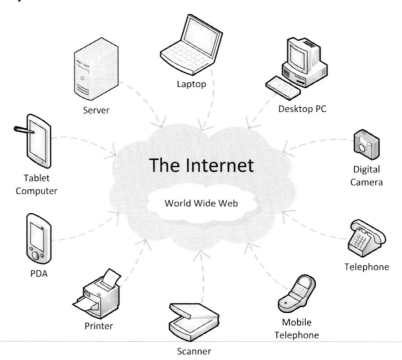

Most people use the Internet to access the **World Wide Web** (WWW). This is the name given to a vast collection of interconnected files called **web pages**. At its most basic, each web page contains information in the form of text and images. However, most web pages today also contain a variety of other multimedia features including video, music and interactive programs.

ⓘ *The World Wide Web is not the same thing as the Internet – in fact, "the web" is just one of the many services that runs on the Internet.*

When combined, two or more related web pages form a **website**. This is a fairly loose term which refers to any collection of web pages that belong together (in the same way that the individual pages of a printed magazine belong together). Most web pages in a website also share the same basic design features and are usually located on the same server.

ⓘ *Web pages are stored on computers called **servers**. These are very similar to your own home, school or college computer, but they are always connected to the Internet and are accessible to everyone.*

Driving Lesson 78 - Connecting to the Internet

▣ Park and Read

There are many ways of connecting compatible ICT devices to the Internet. The easiest technique is to use cables to link computing hardware and peripherals directly to a router/modem (which in turn connects to the Internet). However, it is becoming more and more practical for modern mobile devices to use wireless technologies instead.

  *The connection between a local network device and the Internet is provided by an **Internet Service Provider (ISP)**. This is a third-party communications company that handles the flow of data between your device and the wider Internet. They also supply or rent hardware for connecting to their service such as modems/routers.*

ISPs provide a range of different types of Internet connection. The table below describes some of the most popular types.

Connection	Description
Dial-up	This is an older form of Internet connection which uses a modem connected to a standard telephone line. Although very slow, it is often the only cost effective connection type for people who live in remote rural areas.
Satellite	One of the most expensive types of Internet connection, satellites are useful for people living in remote areas. Although still fairly slow by modern standards, satellite connections are usually much faster than dial-up.
3G and 4G	A popular form of wireless Internet access, 3G and 4G connections provide a direct link between an ICT device and a mobile phone operator's network. Connection speeds are highly variable and depend greatly on mobile phone signal strength. 4G is a newer, faster replacement for 3G (and the lesser-known and rarely used **WiMax**).
DSL/Cable	Popular at home and in small business, DSL (Digital Subscriber Line) and cable connections are wired links to the Internet (using either special telephone lines or fibre optic cables). Because of the high bandwidth, they are usually known as **broadband** connections. Most wireless Wi-Fi routers/modems use DSL or cable connections to access the Internet.
Leased Lines	Popular in big business, these are dedicated wired connections to the Internet with extremely high bandwidth. They are often very expensive!

Driving Lesson 79 - Choosing an ISP

▣ Park and Read

When choosing an ISP to provide an Internet connection, cost and affordability are obvious concerns. However, there are also a number of other important issues to consider before subscribing. For example, is the contract length appropriate (many contracts "lock you in" to a service for 12 to 18 months and they can be difficult to get out of early). It is also important to consider the service's terms and conditions – is that "great deal" really all that great once you factor in hidden charges or bandwidth limitations?

ℹ *Many service providers "cap" their Internet allowances (even if advertised as "unlimited") and you could quickly reach and exceed their "fair usage" limits. At this point your connection may be suspended or extra charges incurred.*

One of the biggest requirements of an Internet connection is **bandwidth** (or **Transfer Rate**). This is basically the speed of your Internet access and describes the amount of data that can be transferred over the connection at any one time. As an example, an average MP3 song that is 5Mb in size would take approximately 15 to 20 minutes to download using a dial-up connection. Using a fast home broadband connection, however, this is reduced to only a few seconds.

ℹ ***Downloading*** *is the term given to the act of copying a file from an ICT device on a network (such as a computer or server) to your own device. For example, when you use the World Wide Web, each web page you visit is downloaded to your computer so that you can view it.*

ℹ ***Uploading*** *refers to the sending of a file from your device to another. For example, you do this whenever you e-mail files to other people or add photographs to a social networking site.*

Bandwidth is measured in **bits per second** (**bps**). As you might guess, this is the number of single bits that can be transferred across a network connection in one second (recall from lesson 7 that a bit is the smallest unit of computer data). Although similar to file size measurements, they are calculated slightly differently, as shown below.

Bandwidth	Description
Kilobits (kbps)	1 kbps equals 1,000 bits per second.
Megabits (mbps)	1 mbps equals 1,000,000 bits per second.
Gigabits (gbps)	1 gbps equals 1,000,000,000 bits per second.

ℹ *Your Internet connection is like a pipe through which data flows like water. The larger the pipe – or bandwidth – the more information that can pass through it.*

Driving Lesson 79 - Continued

Low bandwidth can result in slow downloads and may restrict how you use the Internet. For example, you may not be able to watch videos online or download large files.

Confusingly, ISPs often advertise bandwidth speeds in Megabits (Mb) instead of than Megabytes (MB). A megabit is only 1024 *bits* rather than 1024 *bytes*.

For example, a "10Mb connection" is a very popular home broadband speed. However, consider the following:

10 Megabits (Mb) = 1.25 Megabytes (MB)

At this speed, it would take *at best* approximately 1 minute, 20 seconds to download a 100MB file (not the 10 seconds you might think). In reality, however, it can take a lot longer as users are rarely able to reach their connection's maximum download speed.

Be aware that home users and organisations will have different bandwidth requirements (which may change over time). Consider your individual or business requirements carefully before entering into a contract with an ISP.

Given the ever-increasing bandwidth requirements of the modern Internet, a fast and reliable broadband service is often the best choice for home and small business users who want to download lots of files and watch videos online.

To help you choose an ISP, it can often be helpful to read online reviews by current customers. Watch out for bad experiences or problems such as poor **uptime** *(no Internet availability) or high* **contention** *(a lot of people sharing the same connection with slow speeds as a result).*

Driving Lesson 80 - Wi-Fi Networks

▣ Park and Read

Short-range **Wi-Fi** connections are ideal for people working "on the move" who need to access Internet resources on their laptops, tablet computers or mobile phones. Connecting is usually a simple case of finding a public network and logging on – it really is that easy! In fact, it is so convenient that you can now commonly find Wi-Fi access points (also known as **hotspots**) in many public places, from trains and planes to coffee shops, airports and hotels.

> *Wi-Fi simply replaces cables in a local area network. It is not a type of Internet connection in its own right.*

To make sure only authorised people can access a network, Wi-Fi access points are often protected by a **security key**. This is simply a password used by the owner of the wireless router/modem to control who logs on to their network and, in turn, the Internet. Whenever you try to connect to a password-protected Wi-Fi network, your device will prompt you to enter a valid security key.

> *For security reasons, only connect to secure Wi-Fi networks that require a password. This helps to stop other people from being able to remotely access your computer.*

↱ Manoeuvres

1. *Windows* allows you to connect your computer to a wireless Wi-Fi service quickly and easily. To display the **Connect to a network** pop-up, click on the network icons 🖳 or 📶 in the **Notification Area** on the **Taskbar**.

> *Alternatively, select **Network and Internet | Connect to a network** on the **Control Panel**.*

Driving Lesson 80 - Continued

i *Wi-Fi access is provided by wireless routers/modems that broadcast their name (known as an **SSID**, or Service Set Identifier) for users within range to find. The closer the device, the better the signal strength and faster the connection.*

i *If you are using a computer that does not have Wi-Fi, the feature is disabled or there are no networks in range, you will not see any **Wireless Network Connection** items in the **SSID List**.*

2. Examine the **Connect to a network** pop-up box that appears. If Wi-Fi is enabled and there are networks in range, a list of wireless connections similar to that shown on the previous page will appear.

i *If a network appears with a small shield icon, ⚫︎ⁱⁱⁱ, then this network is "open" and you can connect <u>without</u> a password. However, these forms of network are unsafe and best avoided to ensure the security of your computer and its data.*

i *To connect to one of the networks shown, simply select it and click **Connect**. If the network is protected by a security key, you will be prompted to enter it.*

i *When you connect an ICT device to a new network for the <u>first</u> time, Windows will prompt you to choose a <u>suitable</u> network location for it (i.e. domain, home/work, public). Depending on your choice, Windows will automatically set up, save and apply the best security settings for that type of connection.*

i *Once connected to a wireless network, the text **Connected** appears next to the network's name. In the future, your computer will automatically detect and log on to this network whenever it is available.*

3. Click once on the network icons 🖳 or 📶 in the **Notification Area** on the **Taskbar** to close the **Connect to a network** pop-up.

i *You may need to pay a small charge to connect to and use a public Wi-Fi access point.*

Driving Lesson 81 - Communicating Online

▣ Park and Read

There are many ways to interact with other people online. As the Internet has no international boundaries, you can talk freely to friends, family, colleagues and organisations throughout the world – instantly and with little or no cost. In fact, modern ICT has completely changed the way we communicate with each other and how we do business, giving us access to a worldwide network of advice, debate, feedback, opinion, conversation, support and knowledge.

Aside from the *World Wide Web*, the following table briefly describes the most popular Internet services and mobile technologies available today.

Technology	Description
Chat Rooms	Chat rooms are online spaces that allow people with similar interests to come together and talk about topics which interest them in "real time". Text is typed into a shared window that *all* connected users see.
Instant Message (IM)	With instant messaging (IM) tools you always know when your contacts are online and you can easily start a text or video based conversation with them. These tools are very useful for communicating with colleagues instantly and can be used to request help and support from others.
E-mail	Short for electronic mail, this basic ICT system for sending short messages and files to other people is still the most dominant form of online communication – especially in business.
VoIP	*Voice over Internet Protocol* (VoIP) software such as *Skype* can turn an ICT device (and optional webcam) into a phone, allowing you to talk to friends, family, colleagues and customers anywhere in the world.
Forums & Bulletin Boards	Businesses and people with similar interests can share their views and post messages on dedicated websites called forums or bulletin boards. These can also be used for requesting help and support from others who are often experts in their fields.
Blogs	A blog (which is short for web-log) is simply an online diary in which you can "post" anything that is on your mind. They are very easy to set up and readers are often able to comment on individual posts.

Driving Lesson 81 - Continued

The Cloud	The "cloud" is the name given to a range of online storage areas and Internet-based tools and services. Popular collaboration technologies such as *Office 365* and *GoogleDocs* operate in the cloud, allowing people to access, create, share and edit files from anywhere in the world using only their web-browser.
Social Networking	Social networking sites such as *Facebook* and *Twitter* allow people to communicate with friends and family online by sharing photos, videos, links and comments. You can also chat with friends in real time anywhere in the world.

 Want to work from home? The Internet makes this possible by allowing you to connect an ICT device to your work's server remotely. Once connected, you can access files and use shared resources as though you were "on site". This is known as working remotely and is becoming increasingly popular.

To connect your computer to a *remote* local area network, a **Virtual Private Network** (**VPN**) link can be created over the Internet. This form of connection is fast, secure and reliable and gives your computer complete access to the files, folders, shared devices and services of a private LAN.

 *A network within a company is sometimes referred to as an **Intranet**. This can have all of the standard functionality of the Internet, from interactive websites to the communication technologies described above, but is restricted to internal use (i.e. people outside of the company are unable to connect to it unless using a VPN with a valid username and password).*

All modern communication technologies require access to telephone or mobile data networks to operate. As a result, connection issues – which are very common in rural areas or during periods of maintenance – can be a serious problem for people who rely on ICT to work remotely.

Driving Lesson 82 - Revision

▣ Park and Read

At the end of every section you get the chance to complete one or more revision exercises to develop your skills and prepare you for your ECDL certification test. You should aim to complete the following steps without referring back to the previous lessons.

↱ Manoeuvres

1.   What is a LAN?

2.   What is a LAN used for?

3.   What is an ISP?

4.   What type of ICT device is traditionally used to connect a LAN to an ISP?

5.   What is the difference between the Internet and the World Wide Web?

6.   Name the five most popular types of Internet connection.

7.   How is bandwidth measured?

8.   Which of the following bandwidths is the best (i.e. the fastest for downloading data)?

     A. 2,000,000bps   **B**. 2 mbps   **C**. 2,000 kbps   **D**. 0.02gbps

9.   What is an "open" wireless network and what precautions should you take when accessing them?

10. Name 3 ways to communicate with other people using Internet technology.

11. What is a VPN and what is it used for?

ℹ️ *Sample answers can be found at the back of the guide.*

ℹ️ *Now complete the **Record of Achievement Matrix** at the back of the guide. You should only move on when confident with the topics and features described in this section.*

Section 10
Health and Safety

By the end of this section you should be able to:

Stay safe and use strong passwords

Identify viruses and other forms of malware

Use antivirus software

Adjust accessibility settings

Understand the importance of Green Computing

Change power plans

Maintain your devices safely

Handle routine IT problems

Work through the **Driving Lessons** in this section to gain an understanding of the above features.

For each **Driving Lesson**, read all of the **Park and Read** instructions and then perform the numbered steps of the **Manoeuvres**. Complete the **Revision** exercise(s) at the end of the section to test your knowledge.

Driving Lesson 83 - Safe and Proper Practice

Park and Read

To get the most out of your own education and employment opportunities, you need to be able to use ICT confidently, safely and securely. For this reason, it is very important that you read and respect the **guidelines**, **procedures** and **IT usage policies** of the organisation or business that you work for. These documents will tell you what you can and can't do with technology and help to prevent damaging, illegal, inappropriate and unacceptable behaviour.

When communicating with other people online – at home, in education and at work – consider the following safety recommendations.

- Always use appropriate language and remember to spell-check your messages (especially where e-mail is concerned).

- Do not trust that people are who they say they are online. This may seem obvious, but people can very easily exaggerate or lie about their identities to mislead you.

- Do not send messages or pictures that are likely to offend the person receiving them (including discriminatory or inflammatory material).

- Never give your own personal or financial details to – or arrange to meet offline – people you do not know.

- Always respect other people's confidentiality and avoid inappropriate or illegal disclosure of information. Do not send sensitive information to others without permission and consider who you "copy in" to e-mails.

Data protection laws protect an individual's right to privacy and require that personal information is kept safe and secure at all times. When working for a business, it is your responsibility to keep other peoples' information safe.

- Avoid downloading and using copyright-protected music, videos, pictures and pirated programs. This is illegal and can get you into a lot of trouble!

Copyright laws protect any original work (text, images, music, videos, software, games, etc.) from being copied, used, altered, distributed or sold without the express permission of their owner. In practice, this prevents you from copying pictures and text found on the web and using it in your own work.

- Finally, when at work or in education, remember that personal use of the Internet is usually not allowed.

If you are in work or education, you should locate and read any organisational guidelines, procedures or policy documents that apply to you.

Driving Lesson 84 - Passwords

▣ Park and Read

To prevent other people (i.e.) from gaining access to your ICT devices, you need to protect them with a **password** or **PIN** (Personal Identification Number). If a device is stolen or left unattended for a time, passwords and PINs will act as your own personal entry codes and stop unauthorised use.

> ℹ️ *As well as a password, most computer systems require the use of a **username** which uniquely identifies a person on a computer or network. Together, these prove a person's identity and **right to access** files and shared devices.*

> ℹ️ *Files and folders have **permissions** attached to them when they are stored on a network. This is simply a list of rules stating who can access the information and how (e.g. read only, modify-only, read-write, etc.). By default, you always have sole, full-control over any files you create or save.*

A good password should be made up from a combination of numbers and both uppercase (big) <u>and</u> lowercase (small) letters. It should also be *at least* 8 characters long.

PASSWORD: e55eNtlAls

> ℹ️ *In IT, a character is a single letter, number or symbol. A good tip to help create a strong yet memorable password is use numbers in place of letters.*

It is a good idea to use a password that you can easily remember, but not one that is easy for others to guess. For example, don't use your name or the word password. The same rule applies to PINs: don't use any easy-to-guess combinations such as 1234 or your date of birth.

> ℹ️ *PIN numbers are usually 4 digits long and only contain the numbers 0 to 9. They are most often used to secure mobile devices or bank cards.*

Always keep your passwords and PIN numbers safe and try to avoid writing them down. It is also good practice to change your passwords and PINs often. Remember: <u>never</u> give your security information to other people and try to avoid using the same details for different purposes.

> ℹ️ *Did you know that the small microchip on a bank card stores the owner's PIN number? When they use the card to pay for something in a shop or restaurant, for example, the number on the chip is checked to make sure that it matches the PIN entered on the card reader (known as **chip and PIN**). This prevents people from stealing and using the card illegally.*

Driving Lesson 85 - Computer Viruses

▣ Park and Read

The most well known and feared threat in modern computing is the **virus** – a small piece of "malicious software" (or **malware**) designed to "infect" and cause harm to a computer. All viruses are man-made and get their name from the way they "spread" by automatically copying themselves onto other ICT devices.

The effects of a virus can vary enormously. Some simply change a web browser's home page, others decrease the performance of a computer and a small few cause real damage to file systems by destroying data and preventing operating systems and programs from working correctly. Even more seriously, some malware can identify private and sensitive information within files and then transmit that data to another person via the Internet.

Along with viruses, some common forms of computer malware you may hear about include:

Malware Type	Description
Spyware	This type of software hides on your computer and interferes with your use of the system. Spyware can also record personal, sensitive data and send that information to another person via the Internet.
Adware	This type of software "pops up" annoying advertisements from the Internet.
Worm	This type of software can damage files on your computer, and like viruses are able to copy themselves to other devices (often via e-mail).
Trojan	These are files that look harmless (for example pictures, documents and spreadsheets) but contain any number of the threats shown above.

All forms of malware are simply small programs that must be "run" to replicate or cause damage. Common sources of malware are "infected" e-mail attachments, Internet downloads (especially executable files with .exe extensions), and pirated CDs or DVDs. In *every* instance, the infected file must be opened or run for it to cause any damage.

Driving Lesson 86 - Antivirus Software

▣ Park and Read

One way to defend against viruses is to install antivirus software. This is a small utility program that runs in the background on your computer and scans all files and incoming data – including e-mail attachments and Internet downloads – for known malware.

ⓘ *Unfortunately, new viruses appear every day. To make sure your antivirus program learns about these new threats it needs to be kept up-to-date. This involves downloading the latest updates (also known as virus definitions), which your antivirus program will usually do automatically.*

Always be careful when downloading files of any sort from the Internet. Unless you completely trust the source of the file, it may contain viruses and other malware that can harm ICT devices or allow criminals to steal information. If you do download a file, scan it first using your computer's antivirus software.

ⓘ *Antivirus software can also be used to scan files "on-demand", including your entire computer, which is useful for checking downloaded files and e-mail attachments before you open them. To do this, simply right-click the file and select the option to scan it with your antivirus program.*

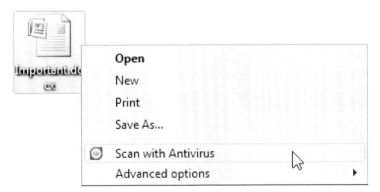

ⓘ *Any malware found by an antivirus program will be automatically deleted or **quarantined** by moving the infected file to a safe location. If a website or file is accessed which is known to contain malware, it will be **blocked**.*

Driving Lesson 86 - Continued

i *Avoid illegally downloading copyright-protected music, videos and programs. As well as getting you into a lot of trouble, these files often contain viruses and other malware.*

At the time of writing, some common antivirus programs include *Norton Internet Security*, *McAfee VirusScan*, *Eset NOD32*, *Trend Micro Internet Security* and *AVG*. Once installed, these programs will watch for and immediately delete any known malware that enters your computer system.

Manoeuvres

1. Using the **Start Menu**, locate the antivirus program that is installed on your computer. This will be found in **All Programs**.

i *If you are using a computer that is not your own (i.e. in a public, business or educational setting), you can ask a person in charge to help locate the antivirus software installed. If the computer does not have an antivirus program you should avoid using it (or suggest one is installed as soon as possible).*

2. The antivirus software installed on your computer will *already* be running "in the background". Start the antivirus program from the **Start Menu** to open its **console** screen where settings can be adjusted and full computer scans performed.

i *An icon for your computer's antivirus software can often be found in the* ***Notification Area*** *on the* ***Taskbar****. This can be double-clicked to open the antivirus console.*

3. Examine the features of the antivirus program installed. Check that the software is fully up-to-date and that there are no warnings.

4. Locate the option to perform a *full computer scan* and examine the options available.

i *Do not run a full computer scan now. This can take a number of hours to complete.*

5. Close the antivirus program's console.

6. Next, open the **Documents** library and navigate to the **Computer Essentials** folder.

7. Experiment with your antivirus program's "on-demand" features (usually accessed via a right-click) by scanning the files and folders present.

8. When you are finished, close any open programs and windows and return to your **Desktop**.

Driving Lesson 87 - Accessibility

▣ Park and Read

A range of advanced accessibility features is available in *Windows* to help people with low vision or limited mobility interact with and use a computer more effectively. Some of these are described in the table below.

Feature	Description
Magnifier	The **Magnifier** feature opens a small window that shows an enlarged view of the screen where the mouse is pointing.
On-Screen Keyboard	The on-screen keyboard allows you to enter text using only the mouse (or other pointing device).
Narrator	This is a **screen-reader** feature which reads aloud any text that appears on your screen.
High Contrast	A high contrast display is easier to view as items and text are more distinct.
Speech Recognition	Using the built-in speech recognition software, you can use your voice to control the computer by speaking commands and dictating text.

⤵ Manoeuvres

1. Open the **Control Panel** and click once on **Appearance and Personalization**.

2. From the options that appear, select **Ease of Access Center** to view a number of settings for users with low vision or limited mobility.

ℹ️ *To help you set up your computer to work best for you,* Windows *features a wizard that can guide you through the various accessibility options available. This can be activated by clicking **Get recommendations to make your computer easier to use**. Alternatively, specific features can be enabled individually using the options below **Explore all settings**.*

3. Examine the various options available on this screen and read the small descriptions that appear below each setting. Find options for enabling each of the accessibility features described in the table above.

ℹ️ *If you feel you would benefit from any of the described features, feel free to enable these now.*

4. Return to the **Control Panel's** main starting screen by clicking **Control Panel Home**.

Driving Lesson 88 - Green Computing

▣ Park and Read

Green computing is the name given to the practice of using environmentally friendly, energy-efficient ICT devices. Today, most manufacturers build hardware with sustainability and energy efficiency in mind, but there are still many things you can do to improve the environmental impact of your ICT use.

Firstly, you should always try to shut-down *Windows* when it is not in use (or place it into a low-power stand-by mode). Secondly, you should set your computer to turn off displays and hard-drives after a period of inactivity.

ℹ *When using other ICT devices such as tablet computers, e-readers or mobile phones, consider energy saving techniques such as reducing the screen's brightness and avoiding over-charging. Always turn off peripheral hardware such as printers and scanners whenever they are not in use.*

ℹ *Think before you print! Unnecessary printing is a waste of resources.*

☞ Manoeuvres

1. With the **Control Panel** open, click once on **System and Security**. From the options shown, select **Power Options**.

2. The screen that appears allows you to select specific **Power Plans** that control how your computer uses energy.

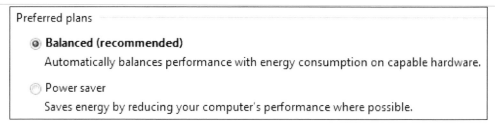

Preferred plans

◉ Balanced (recommended)
   Automatically balances performance with energy consumption on capable hardware.

◯ Power saver
   Saves energy by reducing your computer's performance where possible.

ℹ *Balanced is the recommended and default Power Plan. It seeks to find the best balance between performance and energy usage. Power saver optimises your computer to save energy at the cost of a little performance (and is ideal for use on laptops and tablet computers). The High performance plan, which may be hidden, favours performance over energy saving.*

3. To view the various power settings and observe their effect, click **Create a power plan** on the **Navigation Pane** to create a new **Power Plan**.

4. With **Balanced** selected and **My Custom Plan 1** in the **Plan name** field, click **Next**.

5. Your computer can automatically turn off the display after a set period of inactivity. Select **1 minute** from the **Turn off the display** drop-down.

Driving Lesson 88 - Continued

6. Next, click **Change advanced power settings** to display the **Power Options** dialog box.

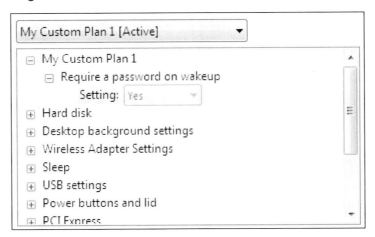

7. Examine the options that can be changed by expanding each power setting shown. Then, using the appropriate option, set the hard disk to turn off after **2** minutes. If available, set the computer to sleep by hibernating after **3** minutes.

8. Click **OK** to confirm the changes, and then click **Save changes** to complete the new plan. Notice that it is now the active **Power Plan**.

9. To see the effect of your new **Power Plan**, try waiting for 3 minutes. After 1 minute the monitor will turn off; after 2 minutes the hard drive will turn off; after 3 minutes the computer will hibernate (if applicable).

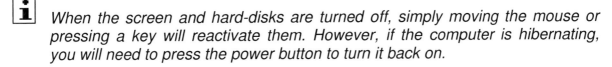

When the screen and hard-disks are turned off, simply moving the mouse or pressing a key will reactivate them. However, if the computer is hibernating, you will need to press the power button to turn it back on.

10. Wake your computer. Then, select **Balanced** again to restore the default **Power Plan** (you may need to expand **Show additional plans** first).

11. Click **Change plan settings** to the right of **My Custom Plan 1**. On the screen that appears, select **Delete this plan**. Click **OK** to confirm the deletion and the custom plan is removed.

ICT equipment and batteries must be disposed of correctly and safely. Many devices contain chemicals which are harmful to the environment and should be taken to a special facility for safe dismantling/recycling. Never dispose of equipment with normal waste and, wherever possible, look to recycle consumables (e.g. paper and printer cartridges) rather than throw away.

12. Close the **Control Panel** and return to your **Desktop**.

Driving Lesson 89 - Routine IT Problems

▣ Park and Read

Although modern computers are very reliable and user-friendly, people often experience problems with them. For example, a program might stop responding when it is being used, a file may not save to a storage device correctly, or a printer can fail to print. When events such as this occur, dialog boxes are designed to "pop up" on your screen to grab your attention.

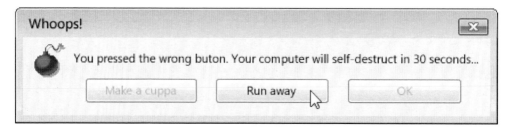

Dialog boxes are designed to explain a problem and suggest possible solutions. Always read the message carefully and make sensible, well-considered decisions.

- If you get a message that a storage device is full when saving your work, delete any unwanted data on that device and try again. You could always save to an alternate location while trying to fix the problem.

- Every once in a while a program will stop working when you are using it, often with little or no warning. In this case the program is said to have crashed. Fortunately, as you learned in lesson 20, you can use the **Task Manager** to force it to close.

- Printer errors are nearly always paper or ink related. If a paper jam occurs, disconnect the printer's power and ease the paper out by hand. If ink is running low, replacements will need to be purchased.

- If a connection to a peripheral device (e.g. a printer) is lost, check its power is on and all wires are correctly and firmly connected.

ℹ️ *Similarly, if a network connection is lost, check your router/modem power is on and all cables are correctly and firmly connected between devices.*

- If a wireless network connection is unexpectedly lost, make sure your router/modem is switched on and working correctly. Mobile computers often have hardware switches that control their internal Wi-Fi and bluetooth devices; be sure to check these are enabled.

ℹ️ *Wireless networks have a short range. If a network connection is lost, you may need to move closer to the wireless modem/router to obtain a stronger signal.*

- If a program routinely fails to work as expected, uninstalling and reinstalling the software will often correct many problems.

Driving Lesson 89 - Continued

 The built-in help system in Windows *will often answer any questions you have. You can access this by selecting **Help and Support** from the **Start Menu** (as you learned in lesson 21). Software applications also have useful help systems which are accessible from within the program when it is running.*

- If your screen is blank, your computer may be in a power saving mode. Press a key or move the mouse to wake it up. If this does not work, try pressing your device's power button.

- If your computer "locks up" (i.e. stops responding completely and the screen freezes), you will need to manually reset it. Hold down the power button for a few seconds until it turns off; then restart it.

 The most useful technique for solving computer problems is to turn your devices off and back on again. You'd be surprised how often this works!

- Messages about virus threats will normally come from your antivirus software. Usually, these simply inform you of updates or the automatic blocking of infected files or websites.

- When downloading files from the Internet or opening e-mail attachments, messages often appear informing you of the potential threat of viruses. Take notice of their warnings and act accordingly.

 If you have any problems with a specific piece of hardware or software, take a look in the manual or help files that came with it. These often contain a lot of useful information about how to deal with and correct common issues.

If you still do not know what action to take to deal with a problem, you should ask somebody else for help. Friends and work colleagues are always a source of good advice, but in some situations you may need to get expert help from your IT department, a help line, or the Internet. When you do this you will need to provide information to help the other person understand your problem; for example, they will need to know exactly what an error message says, when it appears, and which operating system and software versions you are running.

 Internet forums and bulletin boards are often the best place to find advice on computer problems. People are always happy to help.

An advisor may try to walk you through the steps needed to resolve a problem. Follow their advice and, if you don't understand something, ask them to clarify their instructions. If you feel you do not have the skills needed to do what you are told, find someone else who can take over and work through the instructions on your behalf.

 As with most machines, a computer can occasionally break down. If you are unable to get your computer or screen to turn on, consult an expert who will be able to fix or replace any malfunctioning components.

Driving Lesson 90 - Computer Maintenance

P Park and Read

As time goes by and you fill your storage devices with programs, music, videos and files, you may notice your computer becomes slower. Routine maintenance of your system software will help extend your computer's useful life and keep it running smoothly. *Windows* features a variety of useful tools to help.

Feature	Description
Check Disk	The **Check Disk** tool scans storage devices for errors and attempts to fix them.
Disk Defragmenter	The **Disk Defragmenter** tool locates files and folders on a storage device and rearranges them to increase performance.
Disk Cleanup	The **Disk Cleanup** tool lets you get rid of any unnecessary files that use up storage space.

Uninstalling unwanted programs can also help free up storage space and increase your computer's loading times and performance.

Manoeuvres

1.   Click the **Start** button, and then click **Computer** from the right of the **Start Menu**. The **Computer** view is opened which shows all storage devices currently connected to your computer.

2.   Locate and click once on the hard disk drive labelled **Local Disk (C:)**.

*Your local hard disk drive may be labelled slightly differently. In the unlikely event that you do not have a **Local Disk (C:)**, simply choose another device.*

3.   Click the **Properties** button on the **Toolbar**. When the **Properties** window appears, display the **Tools** tab.

4.   Examine the options available here. The **Check Disk** and **Disk Defragmenter** tools can both be accessed from here.

*Note that disk checking and disk defragmenter features can only be used on your computer's local hard drive by an **Administrator**. However, if you have an external storage device connected, you are still able to use these features on that drive.*

5.   Display the **General** tab and click **Disk Cleanup** once to start the tool. A **Disk Cleanup** dialog box appears for a moment.

Driving Lesson 90 - Continued

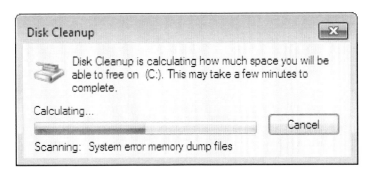

6.   When the **Disk Cleanup** tool has finished calculating space available, a second window appears. Examine the various types of files you are able to delete.

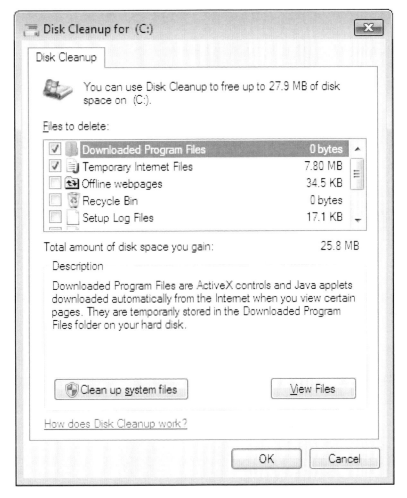

To delete unwanted files, simply place a tick in the relevant checkboxes and click Clean up system files.

7.   When you are finished examining the **Disk Cleanup** window, click **Cancel** to return to the **Desktop**.

Driving Lesson 91 - Cleaning Your Computer

⊞ Park and Read

It is important to clean your computer's hardware to maintain performance and appearance. General cleaning suggestions are given below, but you should refer to a device's documentation for more detailed instructions.

ℹ️ *Remember to dispose of cleaning materials safely.*

Screens

Clean your computer's screen with special screen-cleaning wipes for best results. Alternatively, a wipe with a soft damp cloth is often sufficient (do not use too much liquid). Avoid pressing or rubbing too hard as this may damage the screen's surface.

Keyboards

Unplug the keyboard and turn it upside down. Shake to remove dust, dirt and crumbs. Clean keys with a damp cloth and a mild cleaning agent. Let the keyboard dry fully before plugging it back in.

Mice/Trackballs

Unplug the mouse/trackball and clean with a damp cloth and mild cleaning agent. If the ball can be removed, do so and clean away any dust and dirt from the rollers inside. Dry thoroughly before plugging back in.

CD/DVD Drive

Open the drive and blow compressed air into it to remove any dust. To prevent introducing more dust and debris into the drive, make sure discs are clean before inserting them

Desktop Case

Turn the desktop computer off and unplug it. Clean the external case with a damp cloth and mild cleaning agent. If you are able to remove the side of the case, use compressed air to clean dust from vents, fans, ports, internal components and circuit boards. Use short, controlled bursts of air.

ℹ️ *Laptop, netbook and tablet computers are more complex than desktop computers and should only be opened by qualified technicians.*

ℹ️ *Always turn off and unplug your computer before attempting to open or clean it. It is also advisable to leave the device for at least 30 minutes to allow components to cool. Try to avoid touching any of the internal circuitry.*

ℹ️ *Never use a vacuum to clean a computer as this can damage the device.*

Driving Lesson 92 - Revision

▣ Park and Read

At the end of every section you get the chance to complete one or more revision exercises to develop your skills and prepare you for your ECDL certification test. You should aim to complete the following steps without referring back to the previous lessons.

↱ Manoeuvres

1.   Which of the following passwords is the strongest and why?

     A: password   **B**: HassanKhan   **C**: HKhan3487   **D**: 3487

2.   Name the five most common types of malware that can affect a computer.

3.   Can a virus suddenly appear on a computer?

4.   Name the most common ways that malware is able to "infect" a computer.

5.   Explain the difference between malware and a bug.

6.   What can be done to help protect your computer against malware?

7.   Why is it important to update anti-virus software on a regular basis?

8.   If your computer is working okay is it safe to assume it is not infected with malware?

9.   Name two accessibility features that could help a person with low vision use *Windows*.

10. What is green computing and why is it important?

ℹ️ *Sample answers can be found at the back of the guide.*

ℹ️ *Now complete the **Record of Achievement Matrix** at the back of the guide. You should only move on when confident with the topics and features described in this section.*

Answers

Driving Lesson 1

1. No. The term ICT refers to any device or computer program that creates, stores or uses digital information. Other examples include games consoles, programs and apps, Internet websites and services, mobile devices, and peripherals such as printers, keyboards and mice.

Driving Lesson 7

1. The smallest unit of memory is a bit.
2. There are 8 bits in a byte.
3. There are 1024 kilobytes in a megabyte.
4. There are 1024 megabytes in a gigabyte.
5. There are 1048576 kilobytes in a gigabyte (1024x1024).

Driving Lesson 11

1. Information and Communication Technology.
2. Examples include desktop, laptop, tablet and netbook computers. Modern smart phones and other feature-rich ICT devices could also be considered computing devices.
3. Personal Computer.
4. Hardware refers to any piece of physical technology. Examples include digital cameras, smart phones, MP3 players, desktop, laptop and tablet computers, and internal/external components.
5. Processor and memory.
6. Random Access Memory.
7. Examples include hard disk drives, solid state drives, CD/DVDs, USB memory sticks, flash memory cards and network/cloud storage locations.
8. A peripheral is any optional ICT device that can be connected to a computer. Examples include printers, scanners, keyboards, mice and other external USB devices.
9. Software describes a "program" of instructions that tell an ICT device what to do, how to do it, and when. Software is "run" on a device to perform a specific function, from scanning a file for viruses to providing all of the features of a word processing application.
10. An operating system controls all of the hardware inside of a device, automatically managing memory and data storage and providing the look, feel and functionality of the user-interface. It also allows the user to organise files into folders, start programs and manage a device's settings.
11. When using a desktop computer it is important to set up your workspace correctly. Firstly, the top of the screen should be at roughly the same height as your eyes. Secondly, your chair should be positioned so that

you can sit upright at your desk about one arm's length away from your screen. Your back should be properly supported, your feet should rest flat, and your forearms and hands should remain parallel with the floor. Also remember to adjust the screen to reduce glare and reflections from nearby lights or windows.

12.   Take regular screen breaks, vary activities, maintain a good posture and use simple stretching exercises to stay active.

Driving Lesson 24

8.   54095.

Driving Lesson 40

12.   3.

14.   26.6 KB.

17.   A *PowerPoint* file (.pptx).

18.   7.

Driving Lesson 71

12.   a) Volume control on the **Taskbar** / **Control Panel**.

b) Volume control on speakers.

c) Volume sliders within programs (i.e. *Windows Media Player*).

13.   You should regularly back-up your computer in case of theft, loss or physical, permanent damage to the computer. The back-up should be kept in a secure location free from the risk of fire, theft or flood.

Driving Lesson 75

4.   With the print job selected, click **Document | Cancel**.

9.   Right-click the required printer in **Devices and Printers** and click **Set as default printer**.

Driving Lesson 82

1.   A LAN is a local area network, the name given to two or more ICT devices that are connected to each other.

2.   Devices on a LAN can safely, securely and cost-effectively share data and resources such as files and printers.

3.   An Internet Service Provider (ISP) is a third-party communications company that provides the connection between a local network device and the Internet. They also supply or rent hardware for connecting to their service such as modems/routers.

4.   A modem/router or 3G/4G-enabled device.

5.   The Internet is a global network of linked ICT devices that allow people from all over the world to communicate and share information. The World

Wide Web (a vast collection of interconnected web pages) is the name given to just one of the many services that runs *on* the Internet.

6. Dial-up, satellite, 3G and 4G, DSL/Cable, Leased Lines.

7. Bits per second (bps).

8. D. The other three slower connections have the same bandwidth.

9. An open wireless network does not require a password to connect. These types of network are best avoided as they are not secure.

10. Popular examples include chat rooms, instant messaging, e-mail, VoIP, forums and bulletin boards, blogs, cloud technology and social networking.

11. A Virtual Private Network (VPN) provides a fast, secure and reliable *remote* connection to the files, folders, shared devices and services on a private LAN.

Driving Lesson 92

1. C. This password is the most secure as it uses upper and lower case letters and numbers. It is also more than 8 characters long and is difficult for other people to guess.

2. Virus, spyware, adware, worm, trojan.

3. No. Malware cannot simply appear on a computer system out of nowhere.

4. Common sources of infection include e-mail attachments, Internet downloads, and pirate CDs and DVDs.

5. A bug is an accidental error or fault in a piece of software that prevents it from working correctly. A virus is a small piece of malicious code designed to cause problems, steal information or damage a file system.

6. Antivirus software can be used.

7. Anti-virus software should be regularly updated because new viruses appear every day.

8. False. Not all malware causes performance issues and can run silently in the background.

9. High contrast, **Magnifier** and **Narrator** can all help people with low vision.

10. Green computing is the name given to the practice of recycling and using environmentally friendly, energy-efficient ICT devices and consumables.

Record of Achievement Matrix

The **Record of Achievement** matrix can be used to measure progress through this guide. This is a learning reinforcement process – you judge when you are competent.

Three tick boxes are provided for each exercise. Column 1 should be ticked for **no knowledge** of the subject or topic covered, 2 for **some knowledge**, and 3 for **competent**. A section is only complete when you have ticked column 3 for all exercises.

Tick the Relevant Boxes   **1**: No Knowledge   **2**: Some Knowledge   **3**: Competent

Section	**No.**	**Driving Lesson**	1	2	3
1 Basics of ICT	1	ICT Concepts			
	2	Using ICT Safely			
	3	Your Workspace			
	4	Computing Hardware			
	5	Input and Output Devices			
	6	Connecting Peripherals			
	7	Data Storage			
	8	Computing Software			
	9	Software Licences			
	10	Device Performance			
2 Getting Started	12	Starting a Computer			
	13	Logging On			
	14	The Windows Desktop			
	15	The Start Menu			
	16	Window Layout			
	17	Working with Windows			
	18	Closing Windows			
	19	Starting Programs			
	20	Unresponsive Programs			
	21	Finding Help			
	22	Logging Off			
	23	Shutting Down Windows			
3 Files and Folders	25	File and Folder Navigation			
	26	Folder Views			
	27	File Types and Icons			
	28	Sorting Files and Folders			
	29	Creating New Folders			
	30	Selecting Items			
	31	Copying Files			
	32	Moving Files			
	33	Organising Folders			
	34	Renaming Items			
	35	Deleting Items			
	36	The Recycle Bin			
	37	Item Properties			

Tick the Relevant Boxes   **1**: No Knowledge   **2**: Some Knowledge   **3**: Competent

Section	No.	Driving Lesson	1	2	3
	38	Searching			
	39	Search Filters			
4 Working With Text	41	WordPad			
	42	Entering Text			
	43	Saving Documents			
	44	Opening Documents			
	45	Cut, Copy and Paste			
	46	Printing Documents			
	47	Taking Screenshots			
	48	Recently Used Files			
5 Icons and Shortcuts	50	Default Programs			
	51	Shortcuts			
	52	Arranging Icons			
6 Storage Space	54	Storage Space			
	55	Accessing Storage Devices			
	56	Adding Storage Devices			
	57	Compressing Files			
	58	Extracting Files			
7 Control Panel	60	Control Panel			
	61	System Information			
	62	Display Settings			
	63	Sound Settings			
	64	Date and Time Settings			
	65	Language Settings			
	66	Windows Firewall			
	67	Windows Update			
	68	Backing Up			
	69	Installing Programs			
	70	Uninstalling Programs			
8 Printers	72	Printing			
	73	Printing a Test Page			
	74	Adding a Printer			

Tick the Relevant Boxes   **1**: No Knowledge   **2**: Some Knowledge   **3**: Competent

Section	No.	Driving Lesson	1	2	3
9 Network Concepts	76	Networks			
	77	The Internet			
	78	Connecting to the Internet			
	79	Choosing an ISP			
	80	Wi-Fi Networks			
	81	Communicating Online			
10 Health and Safety	83	Safe and Proper Practice			
	84	Passwords			
	85	Computer Viruses			
	86	Antivirus Software			
	87	Accessibility			
	88	Green Computing			
	89	Routine IT Problems			
	90	Computer Maintenance			
	91	Cleaning Your Computer			